"I Never Get Anything!"

How to Keep Your Kids
from Running Your Life

"I Never Get Anything!"

Thomas W Phelan, Ph.D.

CHILD MANAGEMENT INC

Glen Ellyn, Illinois

Child Management Logo by Steve Roe
Illustrations by Dan Farrell
Edited by Brett Jay Markel

Sales and Distribution by LPC Group

Printed in the United States of America
10 9 8 7 6 5 4 3 2 1

For more information, contact:
Child Management, Inc.
800 Roosevelt Road
Glen Ellyn, Illinois 60137

Phelan, Thomas W., 1943-
   "I never get anything!" / Thomas W. Phelan. -- 1st ed.
   p. cm.
   ISBN: 1-889140-13-9

   1. Parent and child. 2. Child rearing. 3. Child psychology.   I. Title.

HQ755.85.P44 2001   649'.1
               QBI01-201260

to

my family

Contents

PART IV: WHAT TO DO—THE DEVIL AND THE DEEP BLUE SEA

PART V: PRACTICE, PRACTICE, PRACTICE

PART VI: WHAT LIES AHEAD?

Part I

Who's Running
the Show?

What Are These Kids Doing!?

Badgering

Eight-year-old Tommy and his mother, Theresa, are from Chicago. They are visiting Theresa's sister in Minneapolis. Tommy and his mother have always wanted to see the Mall of America. Tommy wants to see the roller coaster and his mother wants to see the stores. So on their first morning Aunt Emily takes them to the Mall.

Things go well until Tommy sees the roller coaster. He goes nuts with excitement.

"Mom, can I go on it? Mom, can I go on it?" Theresa doesn't think these rides are safe; she's sure she's heard of people being killed on them. And *she* certainly doesn't want to ride on the thing , but that would mean her son would have to go by himself.

"No, not today, dear," she replies weakly. As soon as the words leave her mouth, she realizes that her response just implied that she might consent to letting him go some other time. And that in turn implied that she was not totally against his going on the ride in the first place.

Tommy appreciates all this in a heartbeat. The floodgates are opened.

"Mom, just this once! Just this once! Just this once! Mom! Just this

3

once! Just this once! Mom, Mom! Just one time! Just one time! Mom, just this once!" His voice is rising and getting louder. Some passersby are smiling knowingly. Others are scowling. If Mom doesn't let him go, there may be hell to pay—in front of all these people. If she does let him go, she'll be terrified he'll never come back alive.

"Mom! Mom! Just one time! Just one ride, that's all, Mom!!"

Temper

Mrs. Menoni had this to say about her first encounters with one of her new second graders, Loren:

"I got to know Loren last year because of confrontations I had with him on the playground and in the hall. Loren would play roughly with other children, often teasing and even bullying them. Even though I would be careful in confronting him with his inappropriate behavior, he would become very upset. Sometimes he would throw himself on the ground, put his fingers in his ears, close his eyes and refuse to interact at all."

"Other times, when confronted, Loren would simply have a temper tantrum. He would yell at the top of his lungs that I was mean, unfair and had no right to criticize him. Defiance was written all over his face, and he was doing his best to intimidate me. It seemed his reactions were the worst when he didn't expect my confronting him—when my negative feedback, in other words, caught him off guard."

"I was at a loss for what to do. If I confronted him, I produced a tantrum. But I also couldn't let him get away with what he was doing to the other kids."

Threat

It is a hot, steamy day in mid-July. Six-year-old Jimmy is outside in the backyard playing with his dog, Sally. Dad checks out the window and notices that his son is spraying the dog with the hose. Though Jimmy is laughing hysterically, the dog is not enjoying the routine. Unable to escape because she is on her chain, she would rather be anywhere else in the Western hemisphere.

"Come here, Sally. Come here, Sally." Squirt. Laugh.

Dad yells out the window, "That's enough, Jim. She doesn't like that."

The boy does stop—temporarily. But several minutes later Dad hears his son's laughter. Looking out the window again, Jimmy's father sees that the poor dog is drenched. Jimmy is now squirting the animal in the face. The big Lab, generally good natured, is growling. Dad is mad.

"Get in here—right now!" Dad yells. "No!" Jimmy responds. Dad runs out into the yard, grabs his son by the arm, escorts him into the house, and sends him to his room. Both Dad and Jimmy are furious.

Ten minutes later Jim stomps into the family room and announces that he is running away from home.

Dad, still angry himself, says, "Fine!"

Jimmy goes upstairs and packs a small suitcase with some clothes and a toothbrush. Dad watches—saying nothing—as his son noisily drags the suitcase down the stairs, throws it out the front door, and then slams the door behind him. Dad peeks through the curtains. His son is sitting on the sidewalk next to his suitcase. The sun is getting higher in the sky and the temperature—already well above 90—is continuing to rise.

After about fifteen minutes, Jimmy reenters the house and declares, "I couldn't leave because you won't let me cross the street!"

Martyrdom

Eight-year-old Kelly is annoyed. She was just denied the opportunity—by her mother—to go out in the cold and ride her scooter. Kelly thought it was quite warm enough outside. Adding to the injury, her mother then denied her second request: the right to have candy within an hour of dinner.

Kelly marches into the kitchen where her mother is sitting and announces: "I never intend to eat again when you call me for dinner." After her proclamation, she turns, and without saying another word, strides purposefully to her room.

Sure enough, when Kelly is called for dinner at 6:15, she doesn't appear. She is normally a good eater. The family proceeds without her.

Kelly persists until eight o'clock. At that point she suddenly appears and announces to her mother, "I'm ready for my dinner."

Butter Up

It's five o'clock at the Andersen household. Janie is seven and she's a little hungry.

"Mom, can I have a bowl of Lucky Puffs?"

"No, honey, it's too close to dinner."

"Oh please, just a small bowl. I promise I'll eat all my dinner."

"No dear, I don't think so. You know, you usually have trouble finishing your dinner, and this will just make it worse."

Big blue eyes look up at Mom out of an adorable little face. The child's hand gently rubs her mother's arm.

"Please, Mom. Please. I'll eat my dinner and I promise I won't even ask for any dessert."

The child is certainly a cute little creature. And she is usually cooperative, but sometimes her requests can be a little irritating.

"Honey, it's already past five o'clock," Mom says in a pleading tone.

"Just one small bowl, Mom? I'll eat my dinner."

Mom gives in, but she can't escape feeling as though she's been had.

"All right, young lady, but keep it small. And if you don't finish your dinner, don't come to me later telling me you're hungry, cause you're not going to get anything! Understand?"

Physical Tactics

Five-year-old Bobby and his Dad are picking up a few items at their local superstore. Dad is a little nervous taking his son along, because the boy always seems to see a few thousand items that he wants immediately. Sure enough, Bobby spots a package of New Year's Eve party favors—the kind where you pull the string and confetti comes out. For some reason Bobby has really zeroed in on this item today. Dad has no idea how he even knows what they are.

Dad says no to his son's first request because he's afraid the party favors are dangerous and the boy will poke his eye out. But Bobby persists. His voice gets louder. Even louder Dad says "No!" and tells his son in no uncertain terms that that there's nothing more to talk about.

Dad continues to search for a pair of snub-nosed pliers. Just a few moments later his shopping is interrupted by a hissing sound and the scream of a store clerk.

"Hey! What are you doing?! Stop that! Who's kid is this?!"

Dad turns around to see his son holding a can of spray paint. The boy is waving his arms wildly as he sprays the screwdriver display yellow. Drops of paint are dripping from the screwdrivers onto the items displayed below.

What's Happening?

These six children are all frustrated. Life is not giving them what they want at the moment, so each child is engaging in one of the six forms of what we call *testing and manipulation*. Kids use testing and manipulation tactics to try to get their way and also, sometimes, to show their aggravation for not being given what they want. Testing and manipulation by young children is normal, but it is not always easy for parents and teachers to manage. When this challenging behavior by children throws Moms and Dads for a loss, the youngsters can wind up running the house. And when this behavior throws teachers for a loss, classrooms can become chaotic.

Adults need to learn how to recognize the strategies frustrated children use to get their way. Teachers and parents also need to learn how to manage these strategies gently, fairly and firmly.

That's what this book is about.

2

How Far Can I Go?

First-time parents-to-be are optimists. They can hardly wait. Their "expectant" thoughts are dominated by images of the cuddly, affectionate and helpless bundle of joy who will soon arrive.

Sure enough, human infants usually live up to their advance billing. Babies are incredibly cute and engaging; they *are* bundles of joy. The natural charm of infants, no doubt, helps their parents deal with the fact that their freedom to move about the planet has just been greatly restricted. No matter. Parents and grandparents would rather spend hours making fools of themselves trying to induce a smile from a two-month-old.

All too soon, however, two developments—mobility and independent thinking—begin to tarnish the uninterrupted bliss. Infants learn to sit up, roll around and crawl. Many start walking during their first year. Mom and Dad can no longer just put their child down somewhere and expect to find her in the same spot when they come back. Those days are gone forever. Suddenly there is more to worry about and close supervision is required.

In addition to the problems brought on by mobility, as children get closer and closer to two years of age, they start developing minds of their own. They start thinking that some of the things their parents want them to do are not such great ideas: "No, as a matter of fact, I don't want to take a nap right now!" Toddlers also want to do more and more without parental interference. "I'll put the food in my own mouth, thank you!!" When frustrated, these little ones are now capable of whining, screaming and displaying fits of temper.

What happened to that helpless and cuddly bundle of joy? Stubbornness, refusal to comply with parental requests, and outbursts of negative emotion were not a significant part of Mom's and Dad's pre-birth images of what their children were going to be like. The irresistible, captivating and delightful smiles while at Grandma's were expected; the crying and blood-curdling screams in the grocery store were not. Around age two the child can still be fun and affectionate, but there are times when a little monster inside seems to take over.

At this point parents and children are encountering one of the most important and fundamental issues involved in both growing up and parenting. For the kids the issue is: Life can be a lot of fun, but it's beginning to look as though I can't always get what I want. What a bummer! *How far can I go in trying to get what I want, and just how should I go about this task?* Direct frontal attacks do not always work with these more powerful adults. When do I have to wait? Are there times when I should stop, look and listen *now* in order for things to work out better for me *later?*

For Moms and Dads, the corresponding parenting problem is: *When do we give him what he wants and when do we say "No" and stick to it?* When do we insist on proper behavior and exactly how should we go about this "insisting"? Is it right to set limits when these restrictions seem to get the child so incredibly upset? Isn't that emotional upset a sign that something is very wrong? And isn't our job as parents to prevent—rather than to cause—emotional turmoil in our youngsters?

No child cooperates all the time. Though the occasional contrariness and independence of little children is natural, it's a big problem. Some kids will test and manipulate in order to try to get their way. Other children don't bother with testing and manipulation; these kids are simply noncompliant—they seem to just do whatever they want whenever they can. Whichever route the children take, how their parents think about and handle the behavior of their frustrated offspring has a tremendous effect on the parent-child relationship, on each parent's mental health, on the marriage and on each child's ultimate success as an adult.

When parents are unprepared for the inevitable stubbornness and ferocious independence of toddlers, several types of destructive cycles can develop. Some parents simply cave in to their children's ploys. These Moms and Dads have no idea what's happening; they assume that if their child is very upset, either something must be drastically wrong or else they—the parents—are not doing their job right. When parents think like this, the child winds up running the house by the time he is three-years-old. By the time he is five-years-old, he has his parents well-trained and at his beck and call.

Other parents become enraged by their children's oppositional behavior. They think "How dare you contradict or disobey me!" These adults seem to feel that kids should always *want* to cooperate—after all, it's for their own good! These Moms and Dads respond to the children's contrary and uncooperative behavior with the harsh verbal—and sometimes physical—discipline that some writers refer to as "Rambo" parenting. And when their needs and wants are constantly stomped upon by overly aggressive parents, kids with milder temperaments tend to get anxious and depressed over the years. These kids begin to feel that they are bad or worthless, and that they are just a big bother to other people. In social situations they withdraw, anticipating that other people will not like them.

Other children with more feisty dispositions, however, carry the battle right back to their parents. Inconsistent discipline is often the result. On some days the parents cave in. On other days Mom and Dad try overkill and intimidation, and on still other days the arguing is constant. Unfortunately, whether they are formally diagnosed or not, children in these situations often wind up qualifying for what is often called "ODD" (Oppositional Defiant Disorder)—a child who some people describe as a "Super Brat." These kids are angry, argumentative, hold grudges, blame everyone else for their troubles, and never do what they're asked to do without a fight. When they are home, the house seems dominated by their negative presence. Oppositional Defiant children are most often boys, and as many as 10 percent of our youngsters may fall into this group.

As the years go by, and the discipline problem isn't fixed, Super Brats can "graduate" to become Conduct Disordered (CD) teens. Conduct Disorder is the modern euphemism for juvenile delinquency, which results in the mean, nasty, violent, no-conscience kids that concern everyone today. When a Super Brat is also depressed and perhaps even suicidal, you have a walking time bomb on your hands.

Parents who don't know how to manage the testing and manipulation of frustrated kids begin to feel that they are not in charge of their own lives. Said one young mother: "I feel as though my eight-year-old daughter runs the house. Whenever she's home—which is most of the time—it's miserable." Said one 31-year-old father: "The only time I feel like I have some peace and quiet is when I'm at work, and, believe me, my job isn't that easy. But it beats the constant arguing and yelling we have at home."

In addition to ruining the home life of many families, the cumulative effects of parental mismanagement of children's oppositional and manipulative behavior have serious implications for our society at large. Many—though not all—of our problems with nasty and violent adolescents could be prevented if Mom and Dad knew what to do with this difficult behavior early in a child's life.

When it comes to the testing and manipulation efforts of young children, parents need to know two things:

> A. What to think
> B. What to do

What To Think

The bad news is that normal kids do not always cooperate. The good news is that we have now discovered and identified the six kinds of testing and manipulation which are the typical behavior of frustrated children:

> 1. *Badgering*
> 2. *Temper*
> 3. *Threat*
> 4. *Martyrdom*
> 5. *Butter Up*
> 6. *Physical Tactics*

When we say these are normal behavior for frustrated children, we mean that this behavior does not necessarily indicate that there is something wrong with the child who is doing it or that there is something wrong with the parent who is on the receiving end. In fact, children's temperaments vary and some kids push and test a lot more than others.

In this book we'll use the phrases "testing" and "testing and manipulation" as synonyms. There is no well-accepted, sanctioned usage to guide us. Some people think of "testing" as implying more obvious and aggressive forms of youthful persuasion, such as Badgering, Temper and Physical Tactics, while the word manipulation implies less apparent and more subtle forms, such as Martyrdom, Butter Up and sometimes Threat. In any case, "testing" and "testing and manipulation" will refer to *strategies children use to alter the emotional state of adults in order to influence those adults to give the children what the kids want.*

What To Do

Testing is obnoxious but usually manageable. After expecting and recognizing manipulative behavior, Mom and Dad's next job is managing their youngsters' attempts at emotional blackmail *without arguing, yelling or spanking*. In this book we will provide strategies for handling all the testing tactics that kids use.

Wishful thinking will not get you anywhere. Parents cannot will their children into a *State of Perpetual Cooperation and Gracious Acceptance of All Disappointment*. Parental thinking needs to be practical and down-to-earth. Knowing exactly what to expect from frustrated children, and knowing how to handle this behavior, are two of the most important skills parents will ever learn.

3

The Four Choices of
Frustrated Kids

Research has taught us that good parents have two important qualities:
They are *warm* on the one hand, and they are *demanding* on the other.
Being warm means taking care of kids' needs. It means providing food,
clothing and shelter as well as emotional support, sympathy and
companionship. When parents are acting from their warm parenting side,
testing and manipulation are never an issue because the kids are not
frustrated:

> "Mom, can we go out for ice cream!?"
> "Sure, a hot fudge sundae is just what the doctor ordered!"
> "Great!"

Off they go. No problem.

It is when parents act from their demanding side, however, that
testing pops up. The demanding part of parenting means that Mom and
Dad must frustrate their youngsters on a regular basis. Good parents, of
course, do not wake up in the morning and ask themselves, "Now, how can

we go about frustrating our children today?" Yet the job of parenting frequently and inevitably puts Moms and Dads in situations where they must do one or more of the following:

   A. Ask their children to *start doing something*, such as:
   - come in for dinner
   - try harder
   - get ready for bed
   - be nice to other kids
   - get your homework done
   - put your toys away

   B. Ask their children to *stop doing something*, such as:
   - teasing your sister
   - whining
   - watching TV
   - talking with your mouth full of food
   - arguing
   - getting out of bed

   C. *Deny requests* from their children.
   - no you can't have the candy
   - you can't go back outside again today
   - you may not ride the roller coaster
   - you may not sleep with me
   - I can't take you to the store
   - you can't sleep at Michele's tonight

   In other words, good parents expect something from their kids: reasonably good behavior. Good parents also cannot give their children everything the kids want everytime the kids want it. The demanding part of a parent's job, therefore, is to model and prompt, to reinforce good behavior, to say "No," to encourage and praise, to set limits and to occasionally reprimand. When parents shy away from these objectives, trouble results. Mom and Dad may wind up feeling as though the children are running the house: *the adults have been taught how to obey their kids.*

Do Kids Want Limits?

You sometimes hear the phrase, "Believe it or not, kids really want limits." Another version of this somewhat wishful notion appears in statements like "The child's acting out and impossible behavior was really a cry for structure and discipline in his life."

This idea isn't completely true. It is true, of course, that in the long run youngsters are more comfortable in a house where parents have clear, reasonable rules and enforce them consistently and fairly. Under these circumstances the kids are better off whether or not they realize the connection between their parents' behavior and their own well being. In such a home, in addition to feeling cozy, warm and comfortable, children are also developing the critical skill of *frustration tolerance.*

Frustration tolerance is the ability to put up with discomfort or pain *now* in order to achieve some more important *future* objective. It's a beautiful evening and I would like to trash this math homework, but I'd also like to get at least a B in the course. I'd like to slug my brother, but I don't want to upset my mother and be grounded. I'd like another piece of lemon meringue pie, but I don't want to get fat. Successful adults learned high frustration tolerance (HFT) when they were kids. Many unsuccessful adults still show low frustration tolerance (LFT).

Kids are just kids, so naturally they start out at the LFT point. At any one moment, *children want what they want*, and they can be angry and disappointed if they don't get it. Kids generally do not welcome or enjoy adult-imposed limits, and, as a result, the youngsters' unpleasant emotional reactions frequently lead to trouble with their parents. But learning to tolerate frustration is a normal and necessary part of growing up, and as the years go by parents expect their children to get better and better at mastering this difficult and challenging aspect of self-discipline.

So what it boils down to is: Good parenting and good teaching necessarily involve frustrating children on a regular basis. At times you have to ask the kids to start doing something they *don't want to do*. At other times you have to ask the kids to stop doing something they *do want to do*. And finally, there are also times when adults cannot grant children's requests.

When children are being frustrated by their parents or by other adults, the youngsters have basically four "choices." Kids can try to handle the frustrating situation in the following ways:

1. Compliance
2. Negotiation
3. Testing and Manipulation
4. Noncompliance

1. Compliance

"Kathy, it's time to get ready for bed."
"Oh, all right."

When asked to start getting ready for bed, many children start to get ready for bed. When told they can't have the Three Musketeers Bar in the grocery store, many children don't press the issue. They simply continue on, hoping for a better day. In other words, these children cooperate—they comply with the parent's request. Some kids do it with a smile, some do it with a frown, and some just do it because it's part of life.

These kids are learning frustration tolerance. They are accepting the rules and their parents' authority—at least in these instances. Whatever negative emotion they feel, they are able to manage that feeling and then let it go. Parents want their children to learn to cooperate more and more— at home as well as with others outside the home—as the kids get older. (Mom and Dad, of course, also want their kids to be able to stick up for themselves when necessary.)

Cooperating with reasonable parent-imposed limits or demands implies that the following characteristics are becoming a part of a child's growing emotional maturity:

A. Recognition and acceptance of rules and parental authority
B. Ability to restrain emotion
C. Frustration tolerance

There are other times in life, of course, when fun, self-indulgence and free emotional expression are appropriate and even necessary. Going to a party with friends, for example, is not an occasion where emotional restraint and frustration tolerance are usually needed. Neither is going to a movie or to a football game. Learning to find a reasonable balance between self-discipline and the ability to enjoy life is a large part of what growing up is all about. A good parent is part playmate and part disciplinarian.

2. Negotiation

Another option children sometimes have when they are frustrated is to try to negotiate with Mom or Dad. At times this choice can be quite legitimate and it can help the child learn some communication skills. Here are two examples:

Example 1:

"Kathy, it's time to get ready for bed."

"Dad, can I stay up for just fifteen more minutes? I want to finish this game. I'll even take a bath if you let me."

"OK, honey, but I'm holding you to it. Bath time is in fifteen minutes sharp!"

"Thanks, Dad!"

Example 2 (grocery store):

"Mom, can I get a Three Musketeers?"

"Not now, honey."

"How about if we get it now, but I don't have it until after dinner for dessert?"

"Now there's a thought. OK, but I don't want to see it even opened until after we eat."

"Great!"

Like cooperation, talking or negotiation also manifests the following emerging characteristics in a child's self-discipline:

A. Recognition and acceptance of rules and parental authority

B. Ability to restrain emotion

C. Frustration tolerance

If a child's attempt to talk things over is not only appropriate but also successful, parent and offspring can go merrily on their way. That's what we just saw in the case of Kathy's successful bargaining with her father.

There are many times, of course, when talking and negotiation is not an option for frustrated kids. Some of these times involve children's safety. "Do you mind if I run out in the traffic and play for a while?" is not a reasonable proposal. Other nonnegotiable items may involve inappropriate behavior. For example, "We're not going to discuss whether or not you can tease your sister." "We won't negotiate whether you can whine at me." Other times that kids can't be allowed to regularly negotiate involve daily routines, such as getting up and out in the morning, doing homework, and going to bed. If kids were allowed to negotiate going to school every morning and going to bed every night, this lack of structure would not only be tedious, but it would also produce a tremendous amount of conflict. When kids run their parent's lives, however, this kind of unnecessary negotiation occurs all the time.

When a child's effort at negotiation is not successful and a parent sticks with a request (get ready for bed) or with a "No" (no candy bar), the little boy or girl then must pick from the other three choices on our list. It's either back to cooperation or on to testing and manipulation or noncompliance.

3. Testing and Manipulation

A third choice that a frustrated child has is to attempt to test and manipulate her parent right off the bat. Instead of cooperating or trying to talk out a compromise, the child immediately attempts to put some kind of "emotional heat" on the parent so the adult will give the child what she wants. For example:

> "Kathy, it's time to get ready for bed."
> "No! Come on! Please!! I want to stay up for a while longer. I have to finish this game."
> "I'm sorry, honey, it's time for bed. You've got a big day ahead tomorrow."
> "Yeah but I got to finish this game! I'm really close to the end and

I'm winning. It will only take about 15 more minutes!"

"Not tonight. Come on, let's get started."

"Oh, come on! That's not fair! Just ten more minutes! What's the big deal!!?"

"I said not tonight."

"I never get to do anything!"

When kids try testing and manipulation they have six choices: Badgering, Temper, Threat, Martyrdom, Butter Up and Physical Tactics. At the time it is occurring, testing and manipulation behavior manifests the following qualities in a child's emerging character:

> A. Recognition and acceptance of rules and parental authority
> B. Difficulty with emotional restraint
> C. Poor frustration tolerance

With testing the child is still acknowledging that the parent is the boss; the child is not just going and doing whatever she wishes (noncompliance). But unlike cooperation and negotiation, the child is in effect saying to the adult, "Let me see if I can't put some emotional heat on you to give me what I want—now. I may not be the ultimate authority here, but perhaps I can 'persuade' you to change your mind."

4. Noncompliance

Some kids have an extremely difficult time accepting almost any parent-imposed frustration. (There are also, of course, parents who are pushovers; they have great difficulty being demanding.) Of the four choices a frustrated child has, the worst from a parent's perspective is often—but not always—noncompliance. In this case the child simply does what he's not supposed to do (if he has the power) or he simply does not do what the parent requested (also if he has the power).

When asked to get ready for bed, for example, Kathy could say nothing and continue playing her game. This would be an example of simple noncompliance. Noncompliance, obviously, is the opposite of cooperation. *Noncompliance is not testing, though, because the little girl*

is not trying to persuade her parent to sanction her refusal to go to bed.
There is no pressure being put on the parent—no emotional blackmail; the
girl is just not going to bed after being asked. In the grocery store, a
noncompliant child might simply take the candy bar, unwrap it and start
eating, in spite of the parent's refusal to buy it for him. (Don't laugh—
there are kids who have done it.)

There are two kinds of noncompliance: passive and active (or
defiant). When passive noncompliance is involved, a child more or less
neglects to do what the parent wants him to do. The child doesn't take out
the garbage, feed the dog or finish his homework. Passive noncompliance
is often quite innocent, since it is frequently based upon simple forgetfulness
and is therefore somewhat involuntary. A child who gets so involved in
talking on the phone that she forgets her bedtime is being passively
noncompliant.

Active or defiant noncompliance, however, is usually worse and it is
voluntary—all the way. The child's attitude here is "You can't make me!"
or "I'll do what I want no matter what you say!" Young children who are
defiantly noncompliant are extremely aggravating. Adolescents who fall
into this category are scary. The child who eats the forbidden candy in the
grocery store is being actively, or aggressively, noncompliant.

Noncompliance—especially the active type—reveals the following
flaws in the character of the children who are doing it:

> A. Rejection of rules and parental authority
> B. No emotional restraint
> C. Poor (or no) frustration tolerance

One Thing Can Lead to Another!

When a parent makes a demand of a child or turns down a youngster's
request, we have a *mini-conflict* situation. As we mentioned before, how
parents and kids resolve these situations hour after hour and day after day
has a huge impact on family life, marriages, mental health and on the
ultimate maturity of children as adults.

It is absolutely essential, therefore, that parents learn to *efficiently
resolve* the conflicts that result from either (1) their requests/demands of

their children ("Start doing this" or "Stop doing that") or from (2) their denial of their children's requests. A basic parent/child conflict resolution rule is:

The longer a conflict goes unresolved and the more talking done, the poorer the outcome will be.

Learning to resolve conflicts efficiently means fairly quickly as well as reasonably. When these mini-conflict situations are not resolved efficiently, one thing can lead to another. Negotiation attempts, for example, can become testing. Testing, in turn, can lead to noncompliance. In the process, *mini-conflicts* become *maxi-conflicts*.

Let's go back to Kathy and her bedtime.

> "Kathy, it's time to get ready for bed."
> "Oh, all right."

The little girl isn't thrilled, but she does what she's asked to do. The conflict is over. Parental problem-solving skills are not taxed when kids cooperate.

However, when frustrated children choose the next option, negotiation, the process can get a bit more difficult. Here Mom or Dad better have their thinking caps on, because if they don't handle the situation well, negotiation can become testing. In our first example, Dad resolved the situation by allowing his daughter to negotiate a deal:

> "Kathy, it's time to get ready for bed."
> "Dad, can I stay up for just fifteen more minutes? I want to finish this game. I'll even take a bath if you let me."
> "OK, young lady, but I'm holding you to it. Bath time is in fifteen minutes sharp!"
> "Thanks, Dad!"

No problem here either. Even though Dad would certainly not want to negotiate bedtime every night, on this one occasion he was flexible.

From Negotiation to Testing

What if on another night, however, Dad did not feel that flexibility and negotiation were in order? The situation might get dicier. Watch as talking and negotiation escalate into testing:

> "Kathy, it's time to get ready for bed."
>
> "Dad, can I stay up for just fifteen more minutes? I want to finish this game. I'll even take a bath if you let me."
>
> "Not tonight. Come on, let's get started."
>
> "Oh, you come on! That's not fair! Just ten more minutes! What's the big deal!!?" (Type 2, Temper; Type 1, Badgering))
>
> "Why can't you just take 'No' for an answer!"
>
> "I never get to do anything!" (Type 4, Martyrdom)
>
> "You never get to do anything? Oh really? Who took you shopping and out to lunch today? Gee, I think it was me. Or did you forget that already?"
>
> "Just fifteen more minutes!" (Type 1, Badgering)
>
> "You move, young lady, or you'll be sorry!"

Kathy is certainly not cooperating, but Dad is also not doing a good job of resolving the conflict. *The longer a conflict goes unresolved and the more talking done, the poorer the outcome will be.* We wound up here with a very angry father and a very angry daughter—while Mom was cringing in the other room. Later, in private, Mom will question Dad about his lack of flexibility, and then those two will argue. That's the way this family's day will end.

From Testing to Noncompliance

When a conflict situation is not resolved efficiently, bargaining attempts can lead to testing. Testing, in turn, can lead directly to noncompliance. This unfortunate transition can occur when too much time has gone by, too much talking has taken place, and too much anger has been sparked:

> "Mom, can I get a Three Musketeers?"
>
> "Not now, honey."

"How about if we get it now, but I don't have it until after dinner for dessert?"

"Now that's a thought. But I don't think so. Not today."

"Oh, come on, Mom!" (Type 1, Badgering)

"Not today, honey. Hey look! They have that new cereal you like."

"I don't care."

"You don't like it anymore?"

"Don't try to fool me! I just want the CANDY BAR!" (Type 2, Temper)

"Don't yell in the grocery store. There are people all over."

"I DON'T CARE!!" (Type 2, Temper/Intimidation)

"You're not getting any candy, young man, no matter what you do!"

"You can't stop me!" (Type 3, Threat)

"Just who do you think you are!?"

   The angry boy picks up the candy bar and bites off the end of it, paper and all. Then he spits out his first bite and throws the now ruined candy bar into the potato chip display. (Type 6, Physical Tactic)

What a great day for Mom. Noncompliance and public embarrassment all wrapped up in one tidy package. Like this little boy, some children become so frustrated and upset during the course of their testing attempts—and during the course of their parents' inefficient attempts to control them—that the kids eventually disregard rules and parental authority and angrily do what they want. Bewildered parents who let testing drag on and on often do not realize it, but they are actively encouraging noncompliance through their hesitation, ambivalence and irritation.

Time, Talk and Anger

In summary, then, we have seen that part of parenting is being demanding: saying "No" to a child's request or asking a child to do something or not to do something. In these mini-conflict situations kids usually have four options: cooperation, talking, testing and noncompliance. For everyone involved, cooperation or successful negotiation are the best outcomes.

Mini-conflicts can become maxi-conflicts, however, the longer the conflict goes unresolved, the more those involved talk, and the angrier they get. When this happens, the chances of cooperation are minimal and the chances of testing and noncompliance are high. Repeat this sequence hundreds of times over the years and you produce miserable families and kids grow up to be aggravating, immature adults.

How does a parent resolve conflict situations "efficiently"? Before we can discuss that, we need to understand the basics of testing and manipulation. You can't manage a problem unless you know what the problem is and you understand its underlying mechanics.

Part II

The Emotional Clout
of Young Children

4

The Six Kinds of Testing
and Manipulation

Testing and manipulation represent the efforts of children to get what they want. The kids don't want to go to bed, they do want the candy right now before dinner, they don't want to get up and go to school, they do want to hit their sister. When kids test their parents, the children are, in effect, saying that they don't want to cooperate and that they have also given up on negotiation. Though some forms of testing look like negotiation, they really are not. True negotiation is based upon open mindedness and a genuine exchange of information. Testing and manipulation efforts are based upon a single-minded purpose (the child getting what she wants), and testing interactions are also based on emotion, not information or logic.

As we have seen, testing is also different from outright noncompliance. Even when they are testing their parents, kids are still usually acknowledging parental authority, exercising some emotional restraint, and showing some frustration tolerance. Given the fact that testing efforts often stimulate very high levels of frustration and anger in kids, it's amazing that more children do not engage in blatant noncompliance. Most children, it seems, can accept that Mom and Dad are supposed to be running the show.

Contrary to the opinions of many adults, children don't have to be exceptionally smart to engage in one or more of the six different testing behaviors. Unfortunately, these courses of action just seem to come naturally to young children. Kids don't need tutoring to become skilled! Kids test and manipulate in these six ways:

1. Badgering
2. Temper
3. Threat
4. Martyrdom
5. Butter Up
6. Physical Tactics

Type 1: Badgering

Badgering includes the all-too-familiar "Please, please, please!" or "Why, why, why?" routines. Badgering is based primarily on obnoxious repetition. The child keeps after you and after you and after you, trying to wear you down. This is what Tommy was doing with his mother at the Mall of America when he saw the roller coaster for the first time:

> "Mom, can I go on it? Mom, can I go on it?"
> "No, not today, dear."
> "Mom, just this once! Just this once! Just this once! Mom! Just this once! Just this once! Mom, Mom! Just one time! Just one time! Mom, just this once!"
> (Short pause)
> "Mom! Mom! Just one time! Just one ride, that's all. Mom!!"

"Just give me what I want and I'll shut up!" is the basic proposition the child is offering. Don't give the child what he wants, and he'll keep talking till the cows come home.

Some parents attempt to respond verbally to everything a frustrated child says. When this happens, Mom or Dad are in for a very long and frustrating session. Many adults do, in fact, get caught up in a wild goose chase looking for the right words or reasons that will make the child be quiet, but without having to give the youngster what he wants. This goal is usually impossible to achieve.

Lots of children learn, at amazingly tender ages, what we call *The Power of Why*:

> "Michele, we have to go for a ride in the car."
> "Why?"
> "Because I have to get spaghetti sauce."
> "Why?"
> "So I can make pasta for dinner."
> "Why?"
> "Because we have to eat to stay healthy."
> "Why?"
> "Don't you want to be healthy?"
> "No, I don't want to go to the store."

Endless "whys" can drive conscientious parents to the point of distraction, since Badgering often masquerades as innocent (but infinite!) information seeking. And as we'll soon see, Badgering's ability to camouflage itself is enhanced by this tactic's tendency to blend easily with other testing strategies—making for more potent manipulative power.

Type 2: Temper/Intimidation

In frustrated young children who can't talk much, temper tantrums are common. Younger children may throw themselves on the floor, bang their heads, scream bloody murder and kick around ferociously. Many toddlers have worried their parents by holding their breath til they seem to turn blue. Some kids are capable of yelling and screaming for hours, while others can get themselves so upset that they throw up.

In older kids, temper outbursts can involve aggressive verbal attacks, the goal of which is to intimidate the adult target. An aggravated child may swear, accuse you of being a bad parent, or otherwise try to make you feel inadequate or stupid. "All my friends think you guys are nuts!" is an angry adolescent refrain familiar to many adults.

The temper type of testing is the main problem Mrs. Menoni described in her attempts to deal with her student, Loren, in Chapter One: "When confronted, Loren would simply have a temper tantrum. He would yell at the top of his lungs that I was mean, unfair and had no right to criticize him. Defiance was written all over his face, and he was doing his best to intimidate me. It seemed his reactions were the worst when he didn't expect my confronting him—when my negative feedback, in other words, caught him off guard."

The suddenness, duration and intensity of temper tantrums have amazed and bewildered many parents over the years. This tactic makes Moms and Dads think twice before once again saying "No" to a child like this—or before asking him to take out the garbage!

Verbal outburts from small children sometimes throw parents for a loop. For example, one small four-year-old boy, after being told by his mother that it was time for a nap, screamed out in a rage, "I hate you! I'm going to kill you!" Four-year-olds can talk that way sometimes. But his mother, not appreciating this fact and never having heard this from her son before, was horrified. She thought to herself, "Do I really have a homicidal maniac on my hands?"

In order to test out this possibility, this Mom did something unbelievable. She got a butcher knife from the kitchen, knelt on the floor in front of her son, and handed the knife to him to see how far he would go. The boy held the knife up for a second and then started crying. The mother's "experiment" was anything but reassuring, and she immediately made an appointment to have the boy evaluated by a psychologist. Mom's turmoil, of course, would have been much less if she had understood that the boy's temper outburst and comment were not unusual for his age.

Type 3: Threat

Some frustrated children warn their parents of the dire consequences that will ensue if the child is not given what he wants. In our first chapter, that's what Jimmy did when his Dad disciplined him for squirting the dog with the hose. Jimmy threatened to run away from home. "The Day My Preschooler Threatened to Run Away from Home" stories are among parents' favorites. It's surprising how many kids have threatened their parents in this way at some time or another.

One little four-year-old girl, for example, heard from a friend that if you told your parents you were going to run away from home, your parents would tell you all the reasons they loved you and give you anything you wanted. As a result, the next time her parents refused a request of hers, the girl announced she was leaving. Her mother, who knew in advance from the friend's mother that this tactic might be coming, told her daughter that she was free to leave, but the rules were that she couldn't leave the subdivision. The Mom also offered to pack a lunch for the child in case she got hungry. Said the Mom afterwards, "Needless to say, she never made it past the laundry room door. And she has never since told me she would run away again!"

Common threats from children can also include the following:

"I'll never speak to you again!"
"I'm not eating dinner."
"I won't do my homework!!"
"You're gonna be sorry!"
"I'm gonna tell Dad!!"
"I'm gonna tell Mom!!"

Not all the threats kids come up with are funny. In recent years it seems to have become more "fashionable" for kids to threaten to kill themselves when they are frustrated. This statement is never a comment that parents will take lightly, but it is generally less worrisome when it comes from the mouth of a child who is usually in good spirits but who is currently very upset about not getting her way. While shopping with her mother, for example, one little girl, after being denied a purchase, declared that she was going to run out into the traffic if Mom didn't buy her what she wanted.

Whatever the exact content of the threat, the basic message from the child is the same: something bad is going to happen unless you give me what I want.

4. Martyrdom

Everyone understands how invested parents are in the welfare of their children, and this fact is certainly not lost on the kids themselves. Their parents' constant caring and commitment gives children security, a feeling of being loved, and a sense of self-esteem. These parental qualities also give kids a very effective testing tactic: Martyrdom. Kids learn very early on that hurting themselves in one way or another—or acting hurt—can be a very effective way of influencing the behavior of mothers, fathers and teachers.

In our first chapter, Kelly's refusal to eat dinner after being denied the opportunity to go outside on her scooter was an example of Martyrdom. (Her announcement, "I never intend to eat again when you call me for dinner!" was an example of Threat.) Deliberately not talking (the "Cold Shoulder"), choosing to miss a favorite TV show, or sitting in the closet for an hour are other examples of Martyrdom.

This conversation once took place between a father and a ten-year-old girl who had just been told she could not sleep over at a friend's house for the night:

> Dad: "How was your day?"
> Girl: "Fine."
> Dad: "What did you do?"
> Girl: "Nothing."

The message here is: "You guys aren't even worth talking to after what you've done to me."

In addition to acting them out, kids will frequently verbalize martyr-like sentiments. "No one around here loves me anymore," "I never get anything," and "You like her more than me!" are comments not unfamiliar to parents' ears. Simply crying, pouting and looking sad or teary can also be effective ways of eliciting sympathy for one's cause.

One of the more creative and humorous illustrations of Martyrdom was told to me one day by the mother of a five-year-old girl. It seems that the youngster had just been timed out to her room by her mother for disrespectful language. A few minutes after the girl went upstairs, the mother thought she heard someone yelling outside. When Mom went out to check, she heard her daughter calling from her bedroom window to the whole neighborhood: "I can't breathe! I can't breathe!" The mother wasn't sure how this ploy was supposed to mobilize support for the little girl's cause.

Martyrdom is obviously designed to make parents feel bad or guilty. That's why this tactic may be the hardest of the six for parents to handle. It seems that many parents have a guilt button the size of the state of Wyoming, and all some kids have to do is press it to get their way.

Type 5: Butter Up

The fifth tactic, Butter Up, is different from the other testing tactics in a couple of ways. For one thing, while the other strategies are designed to make a parent feel uncomfortable, with Butter Up the child tries to make you feel good—at least for a while.

"Gee, Mom, you've got the prettiest eyes of anybody on the block." Or, "I think I'll go clean my room. It's been looking kind of messy for the last three months." And then there's always, "You're the nicest Dad in the whole world."

A second aspect different about Butter Up is that it often preceeds a possible frustration that the child is anticipating. Johnny, for example, cleans his room before asking his parents if he can skip his homework and go to a friend's house. Mark, on the other hand, completes all his homework before his parents come home and find out he has given his sister a black eye.

With Butter Up the basic message from child to parent is: "You'll feel really bad if you mistreat or discipline or deny me after how nice I've been to you." Butter Up is intended to be an advance set-up for parental guilt. "You'll feel so good about me, or positively toward me, that you won't have the heart to make me feel bad."

Promises can be used by children as manipulative devices. That's what Janie was doing with her mother in our first chapter when she wanted the cereal before dinner. "Please, Mom. Please. I'll eat my dinner and I promise I won't even ask for any dessert." Some promises kids make are impossibilities. One little boy, while in the process of pressing his father for a new computer, said "I'll never ask you for anything ever again."

Apologies can be sincere, and they can also be examples of Butter Up testing. "I'm sorry, I'm sorry. I said I'm sorry," said one little boy in an attempt to avoid a grounding for the evening.

Some children can be very creative when it comes to using this particular testing ploy. One young lad, for example, was angling for a new bike from his parents. They had said "No" to him a number of times because they just didn't have enough money. One night the boy wrote this poem which he put on his father's plate at the dinner table:

> *Dear Dad,*
>
> *To fly like the birds in the air,*
> *Must make you feel joyous and free;*
> *But if I only had a bicycle,*
> *The ground would be perfect for me.*
>
> *Your loving son,*
> *Billy*

Butter Up manipulation is obviously the least obnoxious of all the testing tactics. Some people, in fact, don't think it should be labeled as testing at all. It is true that Butter Up is often hard to distinguish from genuine affection and genuine negotiation. If a child says "I love you" and then proceeds not to ask for anything, it's probably genuine affection. Another child who asks if he can have a friend over if he cleans up his room well enough may be proposing a straightforward and legitimate deal. But if you've ever heard a parent say, "The only time he's ever nice is when he wants something," that's probably Butter Up.

6. Physical Tactics

From a parent's perspective, this last form of testing is perhaps the worst strategy of all. Here the frustrated child may physically attack an adult, break something or run away. Physical methods of trying to get one's way, of course, are more common in smaller children who don't have well developed language skills. When the use of this type of testing continues beyond age four or five, however, we begin to worry. Some kids have a long history of this kind of behavior, and the bigger the child gets, the scarier their physical strategies get. Our earlier example of Bobby spray-painting the store yellow was an example of a Physical Tactic.

Some parents who use time outs periodically tell us that their children will physically attack them when the parent is trying to escort the child to the room or time-out area. (Any child who is mad enough to assault his parent in this way is certainly not going to go voluntarily to his room!) Some youngsters become quite ferocious, kicking, biting, scratching, pinching and hitting the unfortunate parent, while yelling at the top of their lungs.

Other kids will smash or break things—sometimes even their own possessions. For example, one ten-year-old boy was sent to his room for fighting with his brother. The door to his bedroom happened to be shut when he got to it, so he gave it one of his best karate kicks, cracking the door down the middle. Another lad smashed a coffee mug on the tile floor in the front hall of the house. Unfortunately, one of the larger pieces of the mug went flying into the glass storm door, which promptly disintegrated.

Another physical tactic, running away, is infrequently used in younger children, though, as we have seen, threats to run away appear more often in that age group. One seven-year-old boy used a different version of this idea on his mother, who had just denied his request to go out. The boy snuck down to the basement and hid for two hours, not responding to anyone who called his name. The tactic was effective, at least in punishing his mother, who was beside herself with worry by the time her son reappeared.

Combinations

Most testing by children does not fall neatly into only one of the categories we have just described. Combination tactics manifest qualities of one or more of the basic testing methods. One young man who had been told he could not have his favorite dessert because he did not finish his vegetables, went up to his room, grabbed a model airplane he had just finished, threw it on the floor, and then stomped on it repeatedly. His strategy combined elements of Type 6, Physical Tactics, and Type 4, Martyrdom (it was his own plane). In other words, you might call it a "6-4" pattern, and many would agree that there was also some Temper (Type 2) involved.

A child who sullenly claims "I never get anything" is using Martyrdom only. A child who screams "I NEVER GET ANYTHING!" is using tactic 4, Martyrdom, and tactic 2, Temper, or what you might think of as a "4-2" routine.

Janie's sequence with her mother in her attempt to get the cereal was really a "5-1" pattern, a combination of Butter Up and Badgering. On the other hand, verbal temper tantrums that go on and on would fall into the "2-1" (Temper and Badgering) category.

One five-year-old boy used a unique "4-3" (Martyrdom and Threat) tactic on his mother. Feeling that she had come up with some unpardonable restriction on his activities, the boy informed her, "OK, just for that I'm not going to like egg salad anymore!" The mother in this case was able to avoid emotional devastation from this threat, but she could not help laughing.

What is the most famous and aggravating testing combination? It is the notorious "4-1" pattern (Martyrdom and Badgering), commonly known as *whining*. Whining drives some parents absolutely nuts! In our research with parents of young children, whether you are talking about testing or simply obnoxious behavior in general, whining ranks as the number one irritating behavior.

And now the winner... *Whining!*

Just Below the Surface

The dynamics, or underlying mechanics, of testing and manipulation are simple. As we saw before, testing only occurs in situations where a child is being frustrated by a parent and the youngster, for whatever reason, does not want to use any of the other possible options: compliance, negotiation or noncompliance. The first goal of testing is for the youngster to get his way—the child wants to end the frustration by influencing his more powerful parent to change her mind.

A second goal of testing and manipulation can come into play if the parent still does not give in. Kids will often continue testing behavior for the purpose of *revenge*. Because they naturally feel frustrated and angry about not getting what they want, kids sometimes use testing tactics to retaliate. There is nothing horrible or pathological about this kind of acting up—temporarily the children are simply mad and upset.

Before we go into more detail, three important considerations should be kept in mind. First, in this book we are talking about a child being frustrated by a reasonable decision of a parent acting in the demanding parenting mode. The parent, in other words, is denying a request, setting a limit or asking the youngster to do something that is sensible, fair and in the child's best interest. We are not talking about situations where a child is being frustrated or hurt by parental abuse, either physical or emotional.

Second, it is not quite accurate to say that children "choose" to test and manipulate. The overused word, "choice," more accurately applies to the options of cooperation and negotiation, where some self-restraint and thought are required. Though it is subject to the usual laws of behavioral reinforcement, testing and manipulation (as well as some noncompliance) happens more or less automatically. Initially, though, testing is simply the result of low frustration tolerance and the child's desire to get what he wants right away.

Third, the fact that kids sometimes test and manipulate does not mean that they're all going to grow up to be professional criminals or con artists. It's just part of kids being kids. Some children test more than others, but there's nothing abnormal about this kind of behavior.

To Ride or Not to Ride?

The child who tests wants to get his way, *but he still—at least for the moment—accepts the fact that Mom or Dad has the ultimate authority.* The little one is going to see if he can "persuade" the larger and more powerful human to give him what he wants—in spite of the parent's initial resistance.

To accomplish this feat, the smaller boy or girl has to become something of a motivator. The tool the child will attempt to use on the larger and more powerful adult is the tool of human emotion. It's as if the youngster is thinking, "If I can't make you give me what I want, perhaps I can make you 'want' to give me what I want."

Consequently, the kids will try to create an unpleasant emotional state in their parents. After this unpleasant feeling has been created in the adults, the child will, in effect, be making an offer: "Mom, the way for you to get rid of your emotional discomfort is to give me (or let me do) what I want." If the parent does give the child what the youngster wants, the testing and manipulation will cease immediately. Mission acomplished. If the parent does not give in, the child can continue testing or she can consider the opposite extremes of cooperation and noncompliance.

Let's look at an example: Tommy is Badgering his mother in the Mall of America. He wants to ride the rollercoaster. Mom is afraid he'll get hurt. By his Badgering, however, Tommy is creating other unpleasant feelings in his mother. These feelings include the fear of public embarrassment, exasperation with his repetitive requests, and guilt for saying "No" to something her son wants so much. If these other feelings in Mom become stronger than her fear of his going on the ride, she may think, "Oh, well, it can't be that dangerous" and let her son buy the ticket.

If she makes this decision, Tommy will say "Thanks, Mom! I love you!" and run off happily.

Different testing tactics are "designed" to produce different negative feelings in adults. From the frustrated child's point of view, to get your way it is most effective to stimulate in your parents feelings such as anxiety, guilt or embarrassment. It is less effective for kids to stimulate anger. Generating anger in your parent can be counterproductive, since angry adults are usually less—rather than more—motivated to give in.

Slow Motion Replay

Let's look at the dynamics of testing and manipulation as they play out in a simple conversation between a mother and her eight-year-old daughter:

> "Mom, can I have Jeanie sleep over?"
> "Not tonight, dear, it's too late."
> "I never get anything." (sad look on face)
> "Oh, honey, sure you do! You had someone over just last week."   ,
> "There's nothing to do."
> "Why don't you and I play a game?"
> "No, thanks." (girl pouts)
> "Alright, I'll call Jeannie's Mom. But that's it for a while! I'm getting tired of your constantly having to be entertained!"
> "OK!"

To see what's really going on just below the surface, let's look at a slow motion replay and translation/interpretation of that same scene:

> "Mom, can I have Jeanie sleep over?"
> *Child makes request.*

"Not tonight, dear, it's too late."
Limit setting by parent—request is denied.

"I never get anything." Sad look on face.
First testing attempt: a version of Type 4, Martyrdom, using a wild overgeneralization. Goal is to produce guilt in parent.

"Oh, honey, sure you do! You had someone over just last week."
Child's testing tactic is working. Parent takes child's statement seriously and Mom is now squirming a bit.

"There's nothing to do."
Child senses parent's discomfort and ups the ante with another martyr-like overgeneralization.

"Why don't you and I play a game?"
Parent makes weak attempt at diversion. Child is old enough to see through parent's strategy and doesn't take the bait. Child also senses that parent's discomfort has increased and victory may be near.

"No, thanks." Sad face.
Child goes for the kill with continuation of Martyrdom. Why abandon a strategy if it's working?

"Alright, I'll call Jeannie's Mom. But that's it for a while, OK!? I'm getting tired of your constantly having to be entertained!"
Mom caves in but feels frustrated, knowing she's been had. Now she has to make a phone call she doesn't want to make and have another kid over whom she doesn't feel like worrying about. Mom also is mad at herself because she didn't stick to her guns. But mother at this time would rather feel angry than guilty.

"OK!" Sad mood leaves immediately and child is ecstatic.
Testing successful—another peanut-powered victory.

Summary: The first and chief purpose of testing and manipulation is for a child to get what she wants. She wants to stay up later, have a friend over, not do homework, eat a Twinkie, watch TV or continue teasing her brother. After a parent makes a request or sets a limit, the youngster then tries to create an uncomfortable emotion in the adult.

In our example above, Mom denied her daughter's request to have a friend over. Instead of complying or negotiating ("How about tomorrow?"), the little girl got right to work with testing tactic number four. Her goal was to make her parent feel guilty.

Just below the surface the child is then offering the parent a deal. The child who is testing is, in effect, saying "Look, Mom or Dad, you're making me uncomfortable by not giving me what I want. Now, though, I'm also making you uncomfortable by my Badgering, Temper, Threat, Martyrdom or whatever. Now that we're both uncomfortable, I'll make you a bargain: you call off your dogs and I'll call off mine."

Give me what I want, in other words, and the testing will end. Give me what I want, Mom or Dad, and I'll let you feel good again. If the child's quest succeeds, testing and manipulation efforts will cease immediately. That's exactly what happened in our example.

The Second Purpose of Testing and Manipulation

When parents deny a child's request, ask a child to do something, or ask a child not to do something, many kids at first try to get their way by means of Badgering, Temper, Threat or Martyrdom. Butter Up and Physical Tactics are less frequently used as first choices. Once children realize, though, that the game is over and their parents are not going to give in, many kids will drop the issue and cooperate.

At other times, however, some children will continue testing and manipulation tactics even after they haven't gotten their way and even when they know *for sure* they are not going to get their way. What could possibly be the logic of continuing to try to make your parents uncomfortable? The answer is not so much logic as emotion. The answer is revenge. You, Mom or Dad, didn't give me my way, so now you're going to pay for it.

We saw little Kelly before, not eating dinner and not talking to anyone. By 7 p.m. she has probably given up on ever going out on her scooter for that day, and she is certainly not going to get any candy. So why does she stay in her room? Answer: She is angry and she is going to make the rest of the family pay for her trouble. Officially, the tactic she is using is known as the Cold Shoulder, a variation of Martyrdom.

Before we saw Bobby spray-painting the hardware store. Although at his age he may not realize all the implications of his act (i.e., his Dad will have to pay for the damage), he does know he is mad at Dad for not buying the party favors and he knows that spraying the store is an effective way of getting back at his father. Bobby's "6-2" pattern here combines Physical Tactics and Temper to accomplish the payback.

All testing tactics except Type 5, Butter Up, can be used for the purposes of getting one's way as well as for punishment or revenge. Some older children can do a Cold Shoulder (Martyrdom) for days as a way of punishing their parents. (Some adults can do it for weeks!) As a matter of fact, Types 2 and 6, Temper and Physical Tactics, probably more often serve the purpose of revenge, since these behaviors usually make parents quite angry and less motivated to give in.

In the long run, if adults aren't careful and aware of what's happening, revenge-oriented testing can also serve the purpose of children getting their way. Why? Because revenge tactics are stored in parent's memory banks. Parents think to themselves, "Remember what he did the last time you said 'No' to him? You don't want that to happen again, do you?"

So when we say a testing tactic "works" for a child, "works" can have two meanings. Either (1) the tactic gets the child what he wants or (2) the tactic gets effective revenge. It's easy to tell when a child gets what he wants—the parent just gives it to him. He doesn't have to go to bed, he does get the candy right before dinner, his friend does come for a sleepover.

How do parents communicate to their children that the kids' attempts to punish them are working? Parents can show that their buttons have been successfully pushed in two ways: *by getting very emotional and by talking a lot*. Parental comments such as those below involve both a lot of frustration as well as a lot of useless talking:

"Why can't you just take 'No' for an answer!"

"How many times do I have to tell you!"

"You never get to do anything? Oh really? Who took you shopping and out to lunch today? Gee, I think it was me. Or did you forget that already?"

"WHAT IS THE MATTER WITH YOU!?"

"You move, young lady, or you'll be sorry!!"

Parents who talk in this way sometimes do succeed in intimidating their children into a state of temporary cooperation. These Moms and Dads also communicate clearly that their children have made them very upset. Successful revenge by kids not only rewards the youngsters in the present, but it also sends a message for the future: "Cross me again, Mom or Dad, and this is what will happen to you." It's a message that is not lost on parent or child.

6

Adult Reactions to Testing

Now that we understand some of the basic "behind the scenes" dynamics of testing and manipulation, we can look at some of the things adults do that increase or decrease the level of testing and manipulation that goes on in a household or a classroom. We'll also examine some of the factors affecting testing that are not under direct adult control. The forces that affect testing are all intertwined—they work together for better or for worse.

The level of children's testing and manipulation in a particular situation will depend upon the following:

1. Child and adult temperaments
2. The degree to which adults' thoughts about testing are realistic or unrealistic
3. Adults' effectiveness in drawing lines or setting limits
4. The extent to which the two goals of testing are reinforced and the pattern of reinforcement
5. The sheer quantity of talking and emotion that occurs during times of conflict

We'll organize our discussion of these issues primarily on the basis of adult and child temperament, because the other items on the list are highly correlated with—and often caused by—people's innate predispositions to respond in certain ways. For example, whether an adult has a difficult or a gentle temperament will say a lot about how he is going to behave toward his children. The same is true with regard to difficult and gentle temperaments in kids and the effects of these temperaments on children's reactions to adults. We know that kids are not putty in the hands of their parents; at birth kids arrive already programmed to some degree.

For the purpose of our discussion, let's consider two opposite kinds of temperaments. We'll call these types "Difficult" and "Gentle." Here are the characteristics of each type:

Difficult Temperament	Gentle Temperament
A. High activity level/ restlessness	A. Calm
B. Lower tolerance for frustration	B. Higher tolerance for frustration
C. Quick to respond	C. Slow to respond
D. Jumps into conflict	D. Avoids conflict
E. Intense emotional responses	E. Mild emotional responses
F. Negative response to change	F. Flexible

Lots of individuals, of course, won't fall into either one of these categories. They will be somewhere in the middle. But we'll use our two temperament categories to help illustrate what will affect the amount of testing that occurs in family, classroom and other situations. Using our two classifications, in adult- or parent-child matchups there are four possibilities:

1. Gentle Parent/Gentle Child
2. Gentle Parent/Difficult Child
3. Difficult Parent/Gentle Child
4. Difficult Parent/Difficult Child

1. Gentle Parent/Gentle Child

The match made in heaven! When we have Gentle parents and easygoing kids, conflict will be at a minimum. These people will enjoy one another's company and seek one another out in order to have a good time. Easygoing children are often anxious to please, so the demanding side of parenting is less taxing for parents. Whatever realistic or unrealistic thoughts Mom and Dad might have about testing and manipulation are rarely brought into play. Kids respond to parental requests with a minimum of resistance and they can take "No" for an answer without experiencing high levels of frustration. Both conversation and negotiation flow easily. Parents in these situations are not in the habit of attempting to use high levels of emotion to persuade their children to cooperate, nor are the kids in the habit of directing heavy-duty emotional firepower at their parents.

Here's a typical example:

Gentle Mom: "Kathy, it's time to get ready for bed."
Gentle Kathy: "OK, Mom."

Summary: Gentle Parent/Gentle Child

1. Overall amount of testing: *low*
2. Parental thoughts about testing: *rarely an issue*
3. Drawing the line: *little problem—kids usually cooperate*
4. Reinforcement of testing goals:
   A. Kids getting their way: *infrequent*
   B. Kids getting revenge: *infrequent*
5. Quantity of talking and emotion during conflict: *low*

2. Gentle Parent/Difficult Child

With this combination things get more troublesome. With a Gentle parent and a Difficult child, conflict will be regular, but it will be quickly resolved—usually in the child's favor. These mild-mannered parents often draw the line only in emergncies or other critical situations. Their difficulty setting limits is partly due to the fact that these adults tend to see testing and children's emotional upset as signs that something is wrong.

Since this parent never gets horribly upset herself, she assumes that something must be terribly wrong when someone does get very upset. The more upset the child gets, the more the parent thinks must be wrong. These parents then proceed to worry as follows:

"This is terrible!"
"This shouldn't be happening!"
"My child has to be emotionally disturbed to act like this!"
"I must be doing something wrong—my child shouldn't be so upset!"
"I must be a terrible parent for causing such agitation in my daughter!"
"One or both of us needs psychological help!"
"I've got to do something immediately to end this upset!"
"I certainly hope this never happens again!"

Gentle parents can be pushovers when their kids are the more aggressive sort. While these Moms and Dads don't like conflict, their child is capable of diving into battle headfirst—a temperamental mismatch if there ever was one! The child will enjoy the parent's company, since the parent is often a source of gratification, but the Gentle parent may eventually wind up feeling guilty about frequently not liking his own offspring. The child will talk and the parent will listen, but if the child doesn't get her way in a negotiation situation, talking will quickly escalate into testing and manipulation.

Here's an example:

Gentle Dad: "Kathy, it's time to get ready for bed."
Difficult Kathy: "Ah, come on. No! Just a few more minutes!"
Gentle Dad: "Not tonight, honey. It's a big day tomorrow."
Difficult Kathy: "I said just twenty minutes!"
Gentle Dad: "Listen, dear, you really are going to need some sleep."
Difficult Kathy: "I was just starting to have fun. Now I have to stop.
    I never get to do anything around here!"
Gentle Dad: "Well, OK, but just twenty minutes. Then you promise
    me you won't give me a hard time?"
Difficult Kathy: "OK."

Kathy wins, as usual, and no one knows what will happen in twenty minutes when Gentle Dad's next feeble request is made. Unlike Gentle Kathy, Difficult Kathy's frustration tolerance is not so good, so parental requests and parental "No's" are experienced as major negative events—events to be avoided if possible through the use of emotional persuasion.

Though she overreacts to frustration, Difficult Kathy's tolerance for interpersonal conflict (not frustration but conflict) is higher than her father's—and both of them know it. By means of testing and manipulation tactics, this Kathy is willing to up the ante as far as necessary to get what she wants. She knows that usually Dad will cave in first; in the above example, she didn't have to go too far.

Summary: Gentle Parent/Difficult Child

1. Overall amount of testing: *medium*
2. Parental thoughts about testing: *unrealistic/worried*
3. Drawing the line: *big problem*
4. Reinforcement of testing goals:
   A. Kids getting their way: *frequent*
   B. Revenge: *used by child only when needed*
5. Quantity of talking and emotion during conflict: *parent low, child high*

3. Difficult Parent/Gentle Child

Here's the opposite situation. Where a Difficult parent is raising an easy child, conflict due to parental requests and parental "No's" will be minimal. These parents are not always a lot of fun and often are ornery as well, so an easygoing child will try to stay out of their Mom's or Dad's way. During conflicts talking will be minimal and will usually involve "downward" communication from parent to child. The easygoing child will frequently need—and use—her high tolerance for frustration to stay out of trouble with a parent who has a low tolerance for frustration and who is easily set off.

Like Gentle parents, Difficult parents may also entertain unrealistic thoughts about testing and manipulation, but their thoughts go in a different direction. Whereas easygoing parents tend to diagnose their child with a psychological problem or else blame themselves when testing occurs, Difficult adults simply think the kid is a brat. They get mad. Their thoughts go something like this:

> *"This is terrible!"*
> *"This shouldn't be happening!"*
> *"What's the matter with you!"*
> *"There is absolutely no call for this kind of behavior!"*
> *"This child is spoiled, ungrateful and needs a good swat!"*
> *"I can—and I will—end this rebellion immediately!"*
> *"I certainly hope this never happens again!"*

With parental sympathy unlikely, Gentle kids will rarely verbalize their displeasure with anything their parents do at home, and these children will rarely try to negotiate with their high-strung parent. When dealing with a Difficult parent, the only legitimate option for a frustrated child is the first one on the list: cooperation. Any attempts by a child to talk or negotiate in a conflict situation are looked upon as disrespectful. Testing or noncompliance are virtually unheard of; should the child ever consider dabbling in these behaviors, such experiments run the risk of triggering nuclear parental outbursts.

Difficult parents use parenting by intimidation, or "Rambo parenting." With easy kids, however, these parents don't need a lot of emotional firepower. The kids readily take "No" for an answer and they usually do what they are told the first time.

Difficult Dad: "Kathy, time for bed."
Gentle Kathy: "I'm going."

And she goes—quickly. Whether or not Kathy wants to go to bed is irrelevant. Dad's request may have come 20 minutes early because he is in another bad mood, but no matter—this Kathy's not about to question the authority of this fellow. Unfortunately, the consistent cooperation of easygoing kids is taken by intimidating parents as confirmation of their parenting style: "Look how well behaved my kids are! I must be doing it right." What these parents don't see is the anxiety, depression and low self-esteem their children may be experiencing.

Summary: Difficult Parent/Gentle Child

1. Overall amount of testing: *low*
2. Parental thoughts about testing: *unrealistic/angry*
3. Drawing the line: *no problem—parent often draws line prematurely*
4. Reinforcement of testing goals:
   A. Kids getting their way: *rare*
   B. Kids getting revenge: *occasionally*
5. Quantity of talking and emotion during conflict: *parent high, child low*

4. Difficult Parent/Difficult Child

The combination of a Difficult, live-wired parent with a Difficult, live-wired child is a formula for maximum domestic conflict. This matchup also doesn't bode well for the future. The low frustration tolerance of these parents means that they fire out demands to their kids—and deny requests from their kids—at a high frequency. This is typical: "Pick up your coat!", "Leave your sister alone!", and "Get started on that homework!" alternate with "No, you can't have anyone over!", "It's too late for that!" and "Why do you keep bugging me all the time!" All parental demands seem to be made in a rapid, high pitched and irritated voice. Everything feels like a big deal.

Unfortunately, on the receiving end of these parental ultimatums is a child who is not about to roll over and play dead. This kind of youngster is no pushover—she is wired for low frustration tolerance, quick and intense anger, and a willingness to jump right into any brawl. Difficult parents and Difficult kids can engage in full-scale battle very quickly. Emotions—usually anger and frustration—can go from zero to sixty in just seconds:

> Difficult Dad: "Kathy, time for bed."
> Difficult Kathy: "Just a few more minutes!"
> Difficult Dad: "I said now! Move it!!"
> Difficult Kathy: "I"m right in the middle of this program!!"
> Difficult Dad: "You gonna move or am I gonna have to do it for

you!?"

Difficult Kathy: "FOR CRYING OUT LOUD WHY CAN'T I EVER DO ANYTHING I WANT TO AROUND HERE?!" (Starts to get up.)

Difficult Dad: "YOU KNOW SOMETHING? I'M SICK AND TIRED OF YOUR COMPLAINING ABOUT EVERY LITTLE THING YOU'RE ASKED TO DO!!" (Also starts to get up.)

Difficult Kathy: "OH SHUT UP! WHY DO YOU HAVE TO SCREAM AT ME ALL THE TIME?!"

Difficult Dad: "YOU WATCH THAT MOUTH OF YOURS, YOUNG LADY! I WOULDN'T HAVE TO RAISE MY VOICE IF YOU'D DO WHAT YOU'RE TOLD ONCE IN A MILLION YEARS!!"

Difficult Kathy: "Living in this house sucks! Totally sucks!! I wish I were dead!" (Starts toward bedroom.)

Difficult Dad: "GET UP THERE! NOW!! What are you, deaf?!"

Dad "wins"—on this occasion—perhaps because he is bigger and has a louder voice. His own Type 2 testing (Temper/Intimidation) here overwhelms his daughter's use of the same strategy.

On a different night, though, there may be a different outcome— Kathy may win. Difficult parents have a hard time being consistent with Difficult kids. In the example above, Dad's thoughts were primarily angry thoughts. On another night, his thoughts may still be angry, but enough Martyrdom may creep in to significantly change his approach. The result is this:

Difficult Dad: "Kathy, time for bed."

Difficult Kathy: "Just a few more minutes!"

Difficult Dad: "I said now. Move it!"

Difficult Kathy: "I'm right in the middle of this program!!"

Difficult Dad: "You gonna move or am I gonna have to do it for you?!"

Difficult Kathy: "FOR CRYING OUT LOUD WHY CAN'T I EVER DO ANYTHING I WANT TO AROUND HERE!"

(Starts to get up.)

Difficult Dad: "YOU KNOW SOMETHING? I'M SICK AND TIRED OF YOUR COMPLAINING ABOUT EVERY LITTLE THING YOU'RE ASKED TO DO!"

Difficult Kathy: "OH SHUT UP! WHY DO YOU HAVE TO SCREAM AT ME ALL THE TIME?!"

Difficult Dad: "I WOULDN'T HAVE TO RAISE MY VOICE IF YOU'D DO WHAT YOU'RE TOLD ONCE IN A MILLION YEARS!!"

Difficult Kathy: "Living in this house sucks! Totally sucks! I wish I were dead!"

Difficult Dad: "OK, you want to stay up? Stay up. Stay up all night if you want. I DON'T CARE! I don't know why you can't just give me one little break every now and then. Is that too much to ask of your highness? You know, I try to do the best I can, but I guess it's just not enough, is it? Fine, do what you want. Don't bother listening to your father anymore!"

If Kathy accepts Dad's absurd emotional offer, she wins—tonight. So some nights she comes out on top, other nights she doesn't. She nevers knows, because Dad is inconsistent.

What's the problem with that? With Difficult kids, parental inconsistency makes the youngsters try harder to get their way—why not give it a go if there's always a chance? Testing, emotional upsets and arguing become more frequent and more intense. Inconsistent reinforcement is also known as "random variable reinforcement," and, unfortunately, this pattern is a very powerful one. This kind of irregular, unpredictable reward system can produce remarkably persistent behavior, both good and bad. Pigeons in cages, for example, have been taught to peck themselves to death on random variable reward schedules. Many human beings have gambled their families into ruin for the same reason, their fates tied to the erratic but captivating output of slot machines.

When a parent reinforces testing in this way, Difficult kids become More Difficult kids. Some of these youngsters become the oppositional defiant kids we discussed earlier. And some of these ODD kids later become mean and aggressive conduct-disordered youth.

In situations like the one above with Difficult Kathy and her Difficult Dad, what makes matters worse is that both of Kathy's testing goals get reinforced. Over time the child's goal of getting her way is being rewarded on a random variable schedule, while the other testing goal, revenge, gets regular reinforcement. The reinforcement of testing's second goal means that Kathy, through her obstinate behavior, emotional outbursts and arguing, is regularly getting the satisfaction of punishing her father.

How's that for encouraging mean, nasty and even sadistic behavior towards others? In the example above, Dad is broadcasting—loudly and clearly—how successful his daughter is in driving him crazy. And his daughter is so mad she's enjoying every minute of the sweet revenge.

Summary: Difficult Parent/Difficult Child

1. Overall amount of testing: *high*
2. Parental thoughts about testing: *unrealistic/anger and self-pity*
3. Drawing the line: *inconsistent*
4. Reinforcement of testing goals:
    A. Kids getting their way: *random, variable*
    B. Kids getting revenge: *regular*
5. Quantity of talking and emotion during conflict: *parent high, child high*

7

What Is Not Testing
and Manipulation

There are plenty of times when children are upset or misbehaving that do not qualify as testing and manipulation. Just because emotion or parent-child conflict are involved in a situation does not mean that testing is occuring. When real testing and manipulation is occurring, several things are usually true:

1. The nature of the child's emotional upset is frustration or anger rather than anxiety, sadness or guilt.
2. The frustration that prompts the testing is very recent; it happened not more than a few minutes or hours ago.
3. The child's frustration or anger is directed at the person who did the frustrating.
4. The actions of the child are not straightforward noncompliance; they are geared toward the child's getting his way or exacting revenge.
5. The child's upset is not due to physical pain.

As you can see, it's not always easy to tell what really qualifies as testing and what is really some other kind of behavior. But it's important to try to tell the difference, because the true nature of the child's behavior indicates to a parent or other caretaker what should be done.

1. Other Upsetting Feelings

Nine-year-od Mollie was put in bed 45 minutes ago. She usually goes right to sleep. She comes downstairs looking a little teary and crawls in Dad's lap. When Dad asks what the problem is, she says she's upset that the cat died (The cat died two weeks ago.). Is this testing and manipulation, Type 4, Martyrdom? No. The youngster is genuinely feeling sadness and grief. Her behavior is quite different from her normal behavior. The emotion involved is not anger, and the feeling is not directed at her father. The event she is upset about did not occur in the last twenty-four hours, and Mollie can't be trying to get her way because no one can do anything now about the cat's being gone.

Even very strong expressions of emotional upset do not always mean testing is occurring. Not long ago while in the food court of a shopping mall, I was startled by a loud bang. Before I could identify the source of the noise, I heard the equally loud screaming of a small boy of perhaps three or four. The boy was not hard to locate. The poor youngster's face was contorted with pain, and in his hand he was holding a stick that had pieces of shredded rubber at one end—his former balloon. His screaming, of course, was not testing behavior. It was an expression—about as genuine as they come—of shock and disappointment. In trying to comfort her son, the boy's mother offered to get him another balloon, an offer that probably came before that thought had even crossed the boy's mind.

2. Recent Frustration

Seven-year-old Tim comes downstairs after having been put in bed five minutes ago. He has always been a difficult child to get to stay in bed. He says he's upset because the cat died (the cat died four months ago). Is this testing? Yes. Tim always has some reason for getting up, and tonight it's the cat. On other nights it's "These pajamas itch," "There's a burglar in the basement," or "I feel hot."

Tim's frustration tonight did occur in the recent past—it happened five minutes ago when the little boy was put to bed. The cat's death was not a recent event. And in this instance Tim's behavior is directed at his father—the boy wants to persuade Dad to let him stay up longer.

3. Frustration with Someone Else

Parents aren't the only ones who frustrate children. Teachers, friends, enemies and siblings also can present regular challenges that make children upset. Sometimes—though not always—parents are needed to help children manage these other frustrating situations.

Melissa comes in from outside and screams at her Mom, "Jenny's a jerk!" Two hours ago Jenny, the girl from acoss the street, was Melissa's best friend. Is this testing? The answer is "No." Melissa is not frustrated by something her mother did, she's upset with her friend. The two girls will probably be playing again soon.

Is this a time for the warm side of parenting or the demanding side? It's time for the warm side. Sympathetic listening would be a good idea here. Mom might say, "Why, what happened?" or "Tell me what's going on." When kids are telling you about frustrations that have occurred during their day, most often listening is the best course of action.

Sometimes, however, matters can get a little tricky if the "someone else" the child is frustrated with is the other parent. On a Saturday morning Peter walks in the kitchen and says to his mother, "Dad won't let me go outside and play." Is this testing? It very well could be. If Mom and Dad, for example, are parents who employ the Weekly Cleanup Routine, where a child has to clean his room on Saturday morning before playing on the weekend, Peter's comment could very well be an example of "cross-parent Badgering." This tactic is also known as playing both ends against the middle; it's an attempt to get one parent to give what the other one would not.

A good response from Mom would be, "Have you finished your room yet?" A poor response from Mom would be, "That's too bad. Let me see if I can talk to Daddy." That kind of reply will only encourage the child to continue to attempt to play both parents against each other in the future.

4. Testing vs. Noncompliance

Mom and Dad are sound asleep on a warm summer night. It's two o'clock in the morning. They are awakened by the ringing of their front doorbell. Puzzled and somewhat frightened, Dad goes downstairs to see who it is. He turns on the front porch light, looks out the side window, and is shocked to see two police officers standing on his front porch. One of the men is holding the hand of Dad's four-year-old son, Darren.

Dad opens the door, Darren comes in sheepishly, and the police explain. It seems that Darren had gotten up sometime in the middle of the night, and for reasons unknown to his father, the boy climbed out his window, down a nearby tree, and then dropped to the ground. After wandering around the yard for a while, Darren had gotten bored. So the young lad got ahold of the garden hose, dragged it to the parkway of the front yard, and waited for cars to pass by. There weren't many, but when an automobile did pass Darren would hose it down. Eventually someone reported this activity to the police.

Does Darren's unusual behavior qualify as testing and manipulation? No, for several reasons. Darren had not been frustrated by his parents or any other adult recently. In fact, he had gone to bed, gone to sleep and then woke up. The boy's hosing down cars was not an attempt to get his way or to get revenge, he was simply having fun. What we have here is an unusual example of noncompliance, because Darren was probably old enough to have some idea that he shouldn't be doing what he was doing.

A while back we saw a Mom and her son in the grocery store arguing about a Three Musketeers Bar. The argument ended with the boy grabbing the candy bar and biting off the end. Was this behavior testing and manipulation or simply noncompliance? It was both. His act was partly noncompliance because the boy was doing what he had specifically been forbidden to do: eat the candy bar. But his behavior was not total noncompliance, because he only bit off a piece and then, in anger, threw the rest into the potato chip display. These actions sound more like a "6-2" testing pattern: Physical Tactics and with a display of Temper. The purpose? The second goal of testing: revenge.

5. Physical Pain

Testing and manipulation does not come directly as a result of physical pain. When children are crying or screaming after falling off bikes, hitting fingers with hammers, or banging their heads, they are in pain. Their behavior is not anger at their parents and they are not trying to get their way.

It is not always perfectly clear what really qualifies as testing and manipulation and what does not . When a child comes running in the house screaming because she says she was just clobbered by her brother, it is not always easy to determine how much is physical pain and how much is wanting parent to punish brother . Nevertheless, parents will often be in the position of having to make judgments about such matters. No one is asking Mom or Dad to be perfect or mistake-free. Parents must make their best guess and come up with a response that is fair, reasonable and not abusive.

So far we've looked at the different kinds of testing and their underlying dynamics, and we've also examined how adults sometimes react to this kind of behavior from children. In Part III: What to Think— Romance and Reality, we'll help you think realistically about testing and manipulation, and we'll also help you to become more adept at identifying the different types that kids use. Then, in Part IV: What to Do—The Devil and the Deep Blue Sea, we'll talk about exactly what to do and—equally important!—what not to do when the kids are trying to press your buttons.

Part III

What To Think—
Romance and Reality

8

Parenting:
The Dream and The Job

No first time parents are ever be able to fully appreciate—in advance—the enormity, variability and emotional complexity of the important job they are about to undertake: raising a child. From the moment that first child comes home, it's an entirely different world. A dramatic and permanent revolution occurs in the lives of the new Mom and Dad—a revolution that brings totally new kinds of emotional highs and totally new kinds of emotional lows.

The experience of becoming a parent is an odd combination of excitement and shock. Our human brains prepare us for some of the pleasant and exciting aspects of parenting. Unfortunately, our minds do not do a very good job of preparing us for the difficult and unpleasant parts of the big job that lies ahead.

A Trip to Hawaii

Imagine you're about to take a vacation to Hawaii. The trip is now only two weeks away, but it's something you've dreamed about and looked forward to for the last ten months. You are so excited you can't stand it.

Just exactly what does it mean to dream about or look forward to doing something? If you are like most people, this process is fairly simple. When you "dream" about doing something you run through your mind a number of what we call "heaven fantasies." These are mental mini-movies, complete with visualizations and sound effects, that are essentially predictions of the fun you anticipate having. Heaven fantasies are short, limited in number and entirely positive.

If you are travelling to Hawaii, for example, your brain might spontaneously construct a number of brief, pleasant scenes such as these:

Hawaii Trip: Heaven Fantasies

1. Waking up in the morning and not having to go to work
2. Watching a school of colorful fish while snorkeling
3. Sitting by the pool reading a good book
4. Having a glass of wine by the ocean before dinner
5. Driving around in a rented convertible feeling the breeze in your hair
6. Sitting on your balcony watching the sun set over the ocean

The actual reality of a Hawaiian vacation, however, will involve much more than just a half dozen or so enjoyable experiences. It will also involve lots of unanticipated happenings, positive as well as negative. You didn't anticipate the exultation you felt jogging along the beach in the early morning of your second day. There's also no way you could have imagined the delight you experienced when you ran into an old college friend at your Wednesday afternoon scuba class.

There were also, however, a number of unpleasant things you did not anticipate. Your flight was 90 minutes late taking off and the plane's cabin was stuffy during the wait. Then there was the rude rental car agent who wanted $25 per day for any extra drivers. Your "ocean view" hotel room was partial view—not full—and it faced north, so sunsets could not be seen. And the indifferent woman at the front desk said she couldn't change your room.

"But I'm on vacation," you thought to yourself a few times. "It's not supposed to be like this."

So the reality of your trip to the islands was different from what you anticipated. Not that your pleasant predictions didn't come true. Most of them did, but there was much more to the whole adventure than you anticipated, and there were a number of negative experiences that you didn't think of beforehand. Overall it was still a good vacation, but the actual reality of it resembled the *two* lists that follow:

<u>Anticipated positives</u>	<u>Unanticipated negatives</u>
1. Waking up—no work	1. Flight 90 minutes late
2. Snorkeling—cool fish!	2. Rude rental car agent
3. Sitting by the pool	3. Cell phones going off by pool
4. Glass of wine by the ocean	4. 3 days of rain
5. Driving around in convertible	5. Sunburn on back of neck
6. Watching sunset from room	6. No sunsets can be seen
	from room

Parenting: The Dream

It wasn't so long ago that people had children more or less automatically. Having kids wasn't that much of a decision; it was simply what you did after you got married. It would have felt odd *not* to have kids. Some families were very large by today's standards; in some societies one of the motives for having children was so the kids could help with the work that needed to be done.

Today much of that is different. Although a lot of children are still born out of wedlock, having children today is more of a conscious decision for couples than it used to be. People are even waiting longer to get married, and more couples today are deciding not to have children. And when they do decide to have kids, parents-to-be are choosing to have fewer children—an average of about two kids per family versus the three or more that was common in previous years.

Research tells us that when young women and men today decide to have children, there are several common motives. One is the thought of the warmth and affection that can be given to and received from children. Another is the fun and stimulation that children can bring—Mom and Dad can enjoy some of their own childhood experiences again. Young men and women also feel that having children means being more accepted as responsible and mature members of the adult community. Parents-to-be also think about the sense of accomplishment involved in helping kids grow up, and in teaching and guiding them appropriately.

Some of the important, motivational images—or enjoyable mini-movies—people entertain in their minds when they decide to have children include these:

Parenting: Heaven Fantasies

1. Cuddling up before bed reading a story
2. Watching the baby sleep
3. Taking the kids to Disney World
4. Showing the baby to Grandma for the first time
5. Teaching the youngster how to ride a bike
6. Being needed

The exact images, of course, will vary somewhat from person to person. But the dream of having children and the decision to become a parent will be based upon a limited number of short, positive images. This process is normal and this is how dreams work. For many adults, no doubt, the desire to have children is an expression of some of the deepest biological and psychological motivations of the human body and mind.

Parenting: The Job

As we just saw, any dream/motivation process is something of a setup—a setup for disappointment. Why? *Because no dream can ever live up to its advance mental billing.* By definition, dreams are incomplete and largely—or only—positive. (Note that we're not talking about going to the dentist here. You don't dream about or look forward to going to the dentist.) Research on marriage, for example, reveals that there is usually an initial honeymoon period (before the marriage), and then an inevitable period of disillusionment (after the marriage) as unanticipated negatives take their toll. How far the process goes—and whether or not the couple eventually stays together or divorces—depends a lot on how the two people handle these normal but unforseen problems.

Research has also revealed another disconcerting fact: *marital satisfaction goes down after the birth of the first child*. Nobody, of course, wants to hear that piece of news! If having children were really all that is implied in the usual list of pre-parenting heaven fantasies, marital satisfaction should increase as a couple enjoys the uninterrupted delight of living with kids. In a way similar to the *two* lists that more realistically described the Hawaiian vacation we discussed earlier, the reality of parenting goes something like this:

Anticipated Positives	Unanticipated Negatives
1. Reading a story before bed	1. Son won't stay in bed after story
2. Taking the kids camping	2. Kids fight in the tent
3. Taking the kids to Disney World	3. The two of us can't get away alone
4. Showing the baby to Grandma	4. Grandma exhausted after babysitting
5. Teaching a child to ride a bike	5. Daughter refuses to get on the bike
6. Being needed	6. Child prefers your spouse to you

It is important to point out that the "onset of reality" does not mean that the positive experiences don't occur or that they eventually vanish entirely. On the contrary, the good things usually continue and, fortunately, these good things are also accompanied by other unforseen enjoyable events. The setup for disappointment, however, comes primarily from the arrival of unforseen trouble, such as kids' testing and manipulation.

Some parents, of course, say, "I was never so dumb to think that raising children was going to be a cakewalk. I'm a pretty realistic person. I knew exactly what I was getting myself into." Nice try, but that's highly unlikely. How could anyone possibly anticipate *beforehand* all the different aspects—good and bad—that are going to occur during any of life's more complex and extended experiences, such as going to high school, getting married, attending summer camp, taking your first job, or having kids? You can't.

So dreams are just dreams—crude attempts by our minds to predict the future—and to try to insure the continuation of pleasant experiences. Dreams are a series of brain-produced, incomplete and overly positive images. Dreams are a lot of fun, but you have to be careful with them. Sooner or later, you're better off if you appreciate their limitations.

Dreams Minus Reality = Anger/Disappointment

Dealing successfully with your own children and being a good parent involves praising your children, listening to them and having fun with them. It also involves managing kids' difficult behavior—gently but effectively. Reading a story at bedtime is easy; so is taking the kids to a movie or teaching bike riding. Those activities are part of the reality of parenting. What's not so easy is managing sibling rivalry, deciding what to do with the child who gets out of bed thirty times, or handling the youngster who whines incessantly with very little provocation. These aggravations and dilemmas are also part of the reality of parenting.

A lot of bad parenting, as well as abusive parenting, starts with frustrated expectations. In other words, blown heaven fantasies. Ironically, those parents who have the most trouble managing their anger toward their children stubbornly hang on to their pleasant images about raising kids. In their minds, kids should always be cooperative and enjoyable. Anything else just isn't right. There's no room for the many unanticipated negatives that come along with having children.

Parents who have not successfully made the transition from enjoying the parenting dream to accepting the parenting reality sound like this when they talk to their kids:

"What is the matter with you!?"
"How many times do I have to tell you!?"
"When are you going to learn!!"
"Why can't you just take 'No' for an answer!?"
"That's it! THAT'S IT!! I've had it!!!"
"Do you know any of your friends who behave like you do!?"
"Are you trying to drive me crazy!?"
"What is your problem?"

Statements like these indicate expectations that are off-base—way off base. Underlying these angry verbal blasts are thoughts such as "No other parents have to put up with this. Something's wrong with my kid. Something's wrong with me. This isn't right and it's not fair. Parenting young children is not supposed to be like this."

Yes, it is supposed to be like this. Kids are just kids. They don't always cooperate and they're not always fun. Before we can discuss the six kinds of testing and manipulation that children use to get their way from their parents, we have to make it clear that these behaviors are a normal part of childhood. And managing them well—without excessive anger or abusiveness—is part of the reality of parenting.

9

Think!
Back to Reality

We saw before that most parents-to-be do not anticipate kids' testing and manipulation. When young men and women dream about having children, they think primarily about the enjoyable and satisfying aspects of raising kids—not the different kinds of emotional ammunition that their children might use against them. So when kids' manipulative efforts first appear, it's not surprising that parents don't quite know what to make of these behaviors.

Therefore, parental thoughts about testing and parental temperaments often conspire to produce adult responses that range from the overly aggressive to the overly passive. Parents with high-strung temperaments think testing is totally out of bounds and "shouldn't" be happening, so these adults sometimes respond to their children with intimidation and overkill. Overly anxious parents who are pushovers also think testing "shouldn't" be happening, but they interpret these child behaviors as signs that something is wrong with either them or their children. Then these adults try to end the conflict quickly by giving in.

To handle testing well it's important to *think straight first*. In this chapter we're going to examine some of the inaccurate parental thoughts we ran across before, and we'll show how parents can learn to think more realistically. In a sense, you'll need to run your erroneous and trouble-producing notions through a kind of thought shredder.

Imagine a little boy has just been badgering his father about going outside to play after dark. The parent said "No." After fifteen minutes of the child's badgering, the parent stuck to the "No." At that point the boy had a tantrum on the floor, complete with kicking, blood-curdling howls and a little head banging. When these actions didn't produce the desired result, the youngster wrapped up the session by sobbing and making statements such as "I never get anything!" and "You don't even like me!"

What's a parent to do? Before we answer that question, we need to look at "What's a parent to think?" Below are some of the common mistaken notions parents entertain about testing and some suggestions about how these ideas can be changed *to conform more with the reality of the universe*. We'll group these thoughts by their central themes.

1. Testing Is Unusual

The first group of erroneous thoughts views testing and manipulation by children as odd or unusual behavior. These parental ideas can take the following forms:

> "This shouldn't be happening!"
> "Why can't she just do what I tell her!?"
> "Why can't he just take 'No' for an answer!?"

These thoughts all include the basic idea that testing is weird, unusual and abnormal. Implied in this notion is also the idea that the use of emotional tactics by children is a rare occurrence, and that parents in other households probably don't have to put up with that kind of behavior.

Au contraire, mein sweet. Behavior such as Badgering, Temper, Threat and pouting is normal. Testing behavior is certainly not fun—in fact it's aggravating, but it's a sign that the child is alive and well. Testing and manipulation is the typical response parents get from their children when the parents are acting in the demanding parenting mode—either asking the kids to do or not to do something or, as we saw in the example above, not granting a request.

"Why can't she just do what I tell her!?" Because she's just a kid and she's still learning to cooperate. She'll get better as time goes by. Her frustration tolerance isn't that great just yet.

"Why can't he just take 'No' for an answer!?" Because he's still just a small boy and he's not an expert yet in managing tough times.

2. Testing Is Too Much to Bear

The second group of erroneous thoughts views testing and manipulation by children as extremely burdensome and overpowering. Parents who think this way feel overwhelmed and continually see themselves as at or near the breaking point. These parents become afraid of their children.

This set of parental thoughts can take some of the following forms:

"This is terrible!"
"I can't stand another minute of this whining (or Badgering, Temper, Threat, etc.)!"
"She's going to drive me crazy!"

Make no mistake about it, almost all of the testing tactics children use are unpleasant! Who enjoys being pestered to death, or listening to yelling, or worrying about something getting broken? But, by and large, most testing falls into the "irritating but not awful" category. Testing also feels less appalling to parents when parents don't "overinterpret" it and make more out of it than they should.

Some testing tactics are pretty scary or gruesome, but they are unusual. One four-year-old boy got mad one day when his father refused to let him go along to the store. The lad then threw the cat in the dryer, almost killing it. Another little nine-year-old girl, after being asked to correct her homework, chased her brother and sister around the house with a butcher knife, forcing them to hide in the bathroom. Scenes like these are very upsetting, and they can also be signs that the child involved does have a psychological problem that needs attention.

Most testing, though, is unpleasant, not terrible. And if a parent is saying or thinking, "I can't stand another minute of this whining!", *that parent is almost always not managing the situation well*. It's time to draw the line. More about that later.

3. My Child Is Sick

The third group of erroneous thoughts sees testing and manipulation by children as a sign that something is psychologically wrong with the youngsters. These parental thoughts take some of the following forms:

"My child has to be emotionally disturbed to act like this!"
"This child needs psychological help!"
"No normal kid would act this way."

These parental thoughts involve mental health-related interpretations of the child's testing behavior. If a parent has bought into the first two batches of distorted thoughts—testing is unusual and testing is terrible—the next one follows rather easily: testing and manipulation from my child is a sign of emotional disturbance, and we'd better get a professional evaluation. In our psychologically oriented society, it's not so hard these days for Mr. and Mrs. Freud to reach this conclusion.

Unfortunately, once Mom and Dad start thinking this way, a whole lot of other questions come up: If our child is emotionally unbalanced, what caused the problem? Did we? Or, which one of us did? Is it part hereditary? Can it be fixed? What kind of future will this poor child have? Will he ever be able to marry, be financially independent or have friends?

Time to get back to reality. If testing by frustrated children is normal, then its existence certainly does not indicate psychological disturbance. Normal kids have tantrums. Normal kids badger their parents and sometimes say they hate their parents. Normal kids whine, pout and feel sorry for themselves when things aren't going their way.

So the correct interpretation is: Testing behavior is usually nothing more than a sign that a child is frustrated, trying to get her way, or trying to retaliate for not getting her way.

4. The Kid's a Brat!

The fourth group of erroneous thoughts views testing and manipulation as a sign that the child has an inherently mean and wilfully nasty disposition, and that only a superior, aggressive force will solve the problem.

These parental thoughts can take some of the following forms:

a. "What's the matter with you?"
b. "There is absolutely no call for this kind of behavior!"
c. "This child is spoiled, ungrateful and needs a good swat!"
d. "I can—and I will—end this little insurrection immediately!"

The "My Child Is Sick" group of parental thoughts were what you might consider the "psychological diagnosis/ counseling" interpretation of testing and manipulation: My child is emotionally messed up and needs a good shrink. This fourth set of thoughts, "This Kid Is a Brat!", also involves a "diagnosis" and prescription for treatment, but one that is quite different.

Our fourth batch of thoughts basically contains two ideas about children who test their parents: (1) These kids are brats and (2) Brats should be punished—bigtime. A diagnosis of "brat," of course, is not a diagnosis at all; it is really a judgment, and it is more an expression of anger than any well thought out conclusion. Calling a child a brat is like calling someone an idiot or a jerk. These titles are descriptions of people who are very irritating. Brat, jerk and idiot are most often merely emotional statements that don't explain anything. "Why does he behave like that? Because he's a brat, that's why!" Some people find that answer logically satisfying.

What do you do with brats? You punish them severely, of course. No parent should have to put up with this kind of behavior! Parents who go along with the brat/punishment format are often angry intimidators, yet they will frequently blend in a fair amount of their own martyrlike behavior in trying to influence their children. These angry Moms and Dads use their own testing and manipulation on their children. Though they talk a different story, saying "It's for your own good" or "This will hurt me more than you," the real goal of these parents when they punish their children is not to train the kids but to retaliate for what the kids have done to them. It's simply the second goal of testing, revenge, all over again, but going in a different direction—adult to child.

So let's get back to reality and rethink. First, what about the brat interpretation? Kids, even the difficult ones, are just kids. Kids do aggravating things sometimes when they're frustrated, but that doesn't make them brats, jerks, idiots or total losses to humanity. Many parents forget that almost all children—even the most troublesome—do most of what they're supposed to do. They eat, they sleep, they play, they sit around, they go to school when they don't feel like it. And, yes, they also test and manipulate.

What about the severe punishment idea? Back to reality again. In order to raise their kids properly and give youngsters the best chance for success as adults, parents need to put on their thinking caps. Mom and Dad can't just react impulsively with tactics that are merely adult forms of testing and manipulation. Parents have to honestly answer this question: *When I'm frustrated with my children, is my response really an effort to train them, or is it simply an angry manifestation of the desire for revenge?*

Does punishment play a part in raising children? It's surprising how many people don't know the answer to this question. The answer is "Yes." But, punishment that works is mild punishment, administered only when necessary, and administered with fairness and consistency. Good discipline does not include the furious, chaotic and sometimes abusive responses of adults who are themselves in the throes of parental temper tantrums.

5. Where Did I Go Wrong?

The next group of erroneous thoughts views testing and manipulation by children as a sure sign that Mom and Dad have done something seriously wrong in raising the child. These parental thoughts can take some of the following forms:

> "I must be doing something wrong or my child wouldn't
>   be so upset."
> "I must be a terrible parent for causing such agitation
>   in my daughter!"
> "I've got to do something immediately to end this
>   emotional disturbance!"

When their kids test and manipulate, adults entertaining these thoughts conclude that they are inept parents. When their child tantrums, screams or gives the Cold Shoulder, these parents jump to the conclusion that they themselves are incompetent—even though they may have no idea of exactly what they might be doing wrong. These Moms and Dads have an especially difficult time with Martyrdom, because they can feel guilty at the drop of a hat. Unfortunately, many of these mothers and fathers have seen themselves as generally inept during their entire lives. To them parenting is merely the most recent thing they've messed up.

Parents who blame themselves in this way also tend to assume that the more upset the child is, the bigger the crime they as parents must have committed. These adults see their children as normal and they believe normal children don't engage in super-emotional manipulative efforts. When a blow up occurs, therefore, the only alternative left is to think that the parent is the one at fault.

An interesting side effect of this kind of thinking is that these poor parents want to end the upset as quickly as possible, simply because the cessation of hostilities stops—or at least reduces—their guilt. Thus they tend to give in to their kids too fast and too often. In between testing episodes, Mom and Dad may search their souls trying to figure out what they are doing wrong. Though they may come up with no useful or plausible explanations in the long run, in the short run it always feels better when conflicts end and the anxious self-criticism abates at least temporarily.

The reality of parenting small children is really quite different from what these anxious parents are thinking. In fact, the demanding side of parenting requires that Mom and Dad regularly refuse many of their children's requests, and it also requires that parents ask their kids to do things the children don't want to do—also on a regular basis. In fact, if Mom and Dad are not frustrating their youngsters consistently, Mom and Dad are probably not doing their job correctly—unless they have amazingly cooperative kids. So kids' getting upset, rather than being a sign that a parent is doing something wrong, can also be a sign that a parent is doing something right. Family life is not a democracy, and parents cannot give their children everything the kids want.

Parental hope for terminating conflict quickly, of course, is reasonable, but that hope should be based upon a different rationale. Instead of thinking "I've got to stop the hassle so I no longer feel guilty," parents would do better to think "I want to end this conflict by drawing the line effectively. After that I'll deal with the normal frustration and testing behavior of my kids."

6. The Last Episode?

The last group of mistaken thoughts about testing and manipulation by children involves wishful thinking. These thoughts can take some of the following forms:

> "I certainly hope this never happens again!"
> "Maybe this will be the last time."
> "Maybe it's just a stage he's going through."

Since testing sessions are unpleasant, no parents want to see them repeated. So in some human breasts the hope springs eternal that this conflict will be the last. Maybe the kids will finally see the light. After all, this emotional gamesmanship shouldn't be happening in the first place! Perhaps when school's back in session, or when we're on vacation, or when the child hits eight, or after I'm back in shape, the kids will settle down and cooperate more readily.

This nice thought is not based on reality either. Over the years, in families where Mom and Dad are managing things fairly reasonably, children's emotional attempts to get their way generally diminish slowly but steadily. Eight-year-olds, for example, don't usually throw the kinds of tantrums that two-year-olds do. Most ten-year-olds have better frustration tolerance than most five-year-olds. But testing rarely disappears overnight.

No, this episode today won't be the last one.

10

Name That Tactic!

B efore you can manage testing and manipulation, you have to recognize that testing is occurring in the first place. Parents need to keep in mind that kids' attempts at emotional blackmail are a regular and irritating-but-normal part of family life. As we have seen, adults who forget this fact often misinterpret or overinterpret their children's behavior, and as a consequence they end up mismanaging their youngsters.

Remember that frustrated children have four choices: cooperation, negotiation, testing and noncompliance. It is helpful to be able to distinguish these behaviors from one another because parents often have to respond differently to them. Sometimes children use just one type of response, other times they combine two different alternatives, and sometimes they switch from one response to another.

There is usually little problem distinguishing testing and manipulation from cooperation. (You'd be surprised, though!) But telling testing apart from children's first requests, from legitimate attempts at negotiation, and from noncompliance is not always so easy. Here are a few examples that have been provided to us by some of our readers. See if you can determine what kind of behavior the child is engaging in.

1. Oxygen Deprivation

"My mother-in-law told me this story. When my sister-in-law was small and did not get her way, she'd hold her breath. Sometimes she'd actually turn blue. Her mother got so worried and concerned she went to her pediatrician. He said that by swatting her on the bottom it would shock her into taking a breath without her realizing it. She finally broke her of the habit."

Comment: This is a clear example of testing and manipulation. The child is using a Physical Tactic (holding her breath) when she is not getting her way. The tactic also has martyrlike qualities—she is doing something to hurt herself. So the testing strategy would be a "6-4" pattern: part Physical (6) and part Martyrdom (4). The pediatrician's advice, by the way, is questionable and unnecessary. Leaving the room when the child held her breath would probably work better.

2. Tale from the Trenches

"My daughter was about eight-years-old and wanted to spend the night at a friend's house whom I didn't approve of. I told her she couldn't do it. I was cooking dinner and she came into the kitchen and announced to me that she was going to stand there and watch me until I changed my mind. I simply told her that she had inherited her stubbornness from me, and she could stand there until midnight if she wished. I was not going to change my mind. She stormed off to her room and never said another word about it."

Comment: A case of testing tactic Type 3, Threat. The little girl did not get what she wanted, so she was going to try to make Mom so uncomfortable that she'd change her mind. If the little girl had actually stood there for a while staring at her mother, the tactic might then be "2" (Temper/Intimidation) and "6" (Physical).

3. Young Realtor

"One day Michael came back from playing outside and found that his bedroom was a mess again. Michael liked things a little more orderly, but his younger brother, with whom he shared the room, didn't care at all about tidiness. Michael wrote a note to us. He made two copies, and put one copy under my wife's plate and one under my plate right before dinner. Each page was entitled 'Ten Reasons Why I Should Have My Own Room.'"

Comment: This is not testing. It is simply a first request—a rather sophisticated and humorous first request. Michael is frustrated with his brother, but it's his parents he wants something from. And they have not yet had a chance to frustrate him by saying "No." Michael is proposing a negotiation session with them. Go get 'em Michael!

4. Truth Is Stranger Than Fiction

One day I (the author) was shopping at a small grocery store near our house. I got my shopping cart and entered the store. Right behind me came a young mother with a four-year-old boy. She picked up her son, put him in her own cart, and entered the store. The two immediately went by the bubble gum machine and the boy asked for some gum. The mother said "No" and kept moving.

The little boy went totally ballistic. Screams and blood-curdling howls filled the store. I shopped for twenty minutes, and this little fellow screamed for every second of that time. The mother, amazingly, seemed unflustered as she calmly went about her shopping—her son's mouth less than two feet from her ears the whole time. I hurried along and finally got to the check-out counter.

Into the next check-out lane came the Mom with her screaming son still in the cart. Mom paid for her items and headed back out of the store. With some relief I watched her go. To my undying and eternal amazement, as the pair passed the bubble gum machine, the lady bought her son a piece of gum!

Comment: Definitely testing and manipulation, Type 2, Temper. Sustained yelling in public is a favorite tactic many kids use to destroy parental resistance. Mom's incredible and hard-to-fathom turnaround at the end will go a long way toward ensuring that this lad will continue his unruly and demanding behavior in the future.

5. Bedtime Dilemma

"Our daughter was in first grade, but at night she was still sleeping with us. We had just gotten into the habit of doing this. Now we wanted to break her of the routine, but nothing seemed to work. Talking it over was useless. So one night we went to bed, locked the door, and put a note on the door telling her she couldn't come in.

"Surprisingly, after we turned in, we never heard a sound from our daughter. No complaints, no temper, no nothing. At 4 a.m. I got up and went to her bedroom. Her door was closed, but there was a note on it. In an unusual, very tiny handwriting the note said 'I'm sorry I have to do this. I'm going away.' I went in her room. My daughter woke up.

" 'Where are you going?' I asked. She wouldn't talk.

"I said to her, 'We'd be sad if you went, but you still can't sleep in our room.' "

"The next morning we went on with our lives, and the subject never came up again."

Comment: Here we have a written Threat (Type 3) from the frustrated child, combined with a few touches of Martyrdom (Type 4).

6. Three-Year-Old Teen

"My three-and-one-half year-old son, Jason, was told that s___ was a naughty word and he shouldn't say it. We rented a movie we thought was kid friendly and heard someone say s___. Jason asked me, 'Mom, did he say s___?' I told him yes, but that was very naughty and he shouldn't say it.

"My husband walked into the room. Jason told him, 'Dad that guy said s___. Right, Mom? That guy said s___! (emphasizing the word every time he said it). Dad, that guy was naughty because he said s___. Right Dad?'

"After about five times, he finally quit saying it, but our son certainly made the most of his opportunities!"

Comment: Is this testing and manipulation? No. It's an example of simple noncompliance. This little boy is having some fun doing something he is just learning that he shouldn't do. He's not frustrated with his parents and does not want anything from them. Right, Mom?

7. Strong-Willed Wendy

"One of our daughters is six, ADHD and EXTREMELY STRONG WILLED. When she has acted up and I tell her she has to go to her room, she will often say "I'll obey you now." When I insist that she still go to her room, she refuses. So I double the time because of her attitude. Then she usually runs away and I have to chase her down and carry her to her room.

"Am I doing the right thing? I need to get really good at this because she is EXTREMELY MANIPULATIVE."

Comment: This sequence is a little more complex. "I'll obey you now" is an example of Type 5, Butter Up manipulation. Kids often try to avoid consequences by making promises or apologies. Wendy's next move, not going to her room after she had been told to, is an example of noncompliance. Running away from her mother combines some noncompliance with Type 6 testing, which involves Physical Tactics. This little one is a handful!

8. Oxymoron

"On certain occasions when she wasn't getting her way, our little girl was in the habit of screaming loudly, 'I'm going to kill myself and then run away from home!'"

Comment: An obvious "3-2" combination, Threat plus Temper. There is also a tone of Martyrdom to the girl's presentation, so—if you like numbers—the whole operation could also be categorized as a "4-3-2."

9. All of the Above?

"I had been sick for three weeks and had pretty much let my six-and-one-half-year-old son run the house. When I finally started feeling better, I thought it was time to be the parent again. When my son acted up one day, I told him he had to sit on a chair. My husband is an over-the-road truck driver and was not home to help.

"Well, my son figured he was no longer a little boy and at six and one half he wanted to show me he was the boss and make me listen to him. I had to escort him to the time-out chair, and then for the next twenty minutes he used every variation of behavior to get out of that corner. He never did get out of that chair but he told me how unfair and mean I was, and just as quickly he would start hitting his legs and saying how naughty he was. When I continued to ignore this and walked through the room he was in, he started telling me how much he loved me and blew me kisses. When I ignored that, he started crying and begging me to be fair and let him out of the corner because he did not belong there. He continued to use all of these methods over and over again till he finally said, in a calm voice, 'OK, I'm ready to come out now.'

"The timer didn't go off for six more minutes, though. After his timer went off, he came to find me, hug me and tell me he was sorry."

Comment: Whew! A "6-5-4-2-1" pattern if there ever was one! This kid used every single testing tactic except Threat. What is amazing is that, with all that energy, he did not ever engage in simple noncompliance— getting off the chair. It would have been easy to do and lots of kids have done just that. One reason this boy did not graduate from testing to noncompliance was that his mother handled the situation so well. She stuck to her guns, without being abusive, and she also did not make her son angrier by engaging in a lot of stupid, useless and provocative chatter. A+ for this parent!

10. Pint-Sized Grumbler

"My son had been counted out and was told to go to his room for five minutes. On the way up we could hear him saying in a fairly loud voice how unfair this was and how he was never coming out of the room again as long as he lived. It was also his opinion that no other children in the entire world were mistreated to the extent that he was. After he got to the room and closed the door, we could no longer hear what he was saying."

Comment: An example of cooperation plus a little testing along the lines of Martyrdom and Threat. The legs are heading toward the room (cooperation) while the mouth is complaining about the whole procedure (testing). As long as the child goes to the room, his angry verbal ramblings can be ignored unless they become exceptionally nasty or vicious.

Take a moment to think about what your children do when they are frustrated with you. Naming each testing tactic (don't forget combinations!)

is an important step in thinking clearly and keeping things in perspective. This brief exercise will also help you with what is perhaps the most critical element in the management process: controlling the amount of—and the nature of—your talking.

Test Your Diagnostic Skill

Now you are ready to take our Testing & Manipulation Multiple Choice Test! Below are short examples of things that kids sometimes say or do when they are frustrated and want to either get their way or retaliate for not getting their way. Look at each item and pick which of the six tactics the child might be using. Answers may vary some (but not a whole lot) because we are not describing each situation in detail. And don't forget that some examples may represent combinations of two or more testing strategies.

A. When a frustrated child says or does this...

"I'm not going to like you anymore."

it's probably...

1. Badgering
2. Temper/Intimidation
3. Threat
4. Martyrdom
5. Butter Up
6. Physical Tactic

B. When a frustrated child says or does this...

"I hate you!"

it's probably...

1. Badgering
2. Temper/Intimidation
3. Threat

4. Martyrdom
5. Butter Up
6. Physical Tactic

C. When a frustrated child says or does this...

"Please... please... please... come on... please!"

it's probably...

1. Badgering
2. Temper/Intimidation
3. Threat
4. Martyrdom
5. Butter Up
6. Physical Tactic

D. When a frustrated child says or does this...

Swears

it's probably...

1. Badgering
2. Temper/Intimidation
3. Threat
4. Martyrdom
5. Butter Up
6. Physical Tactic

E. When a frustrated child says or does this...

"I promise I'll never do it again."

it's probably...

1. Badgering
2. Temper/Intimidation
3. Threat

4. Martyrdom

5. Butter Up

6. Physical Tactic

F. When a frustrated child says or does this...

"You don't love me anymore."

it's probably...

1. Badgering

2. Temper/Intimidation

3. Threat

4. Martyrdom

5. Butter Up

6. Physical Tactic

G. When a frustrated child says or does this...

"I'm sorry. I'm sorry. I'm sorry! I'm sorry!"

it's probably...

1. Badgering

2. Temper/Intimidation

3. Threat

4. Martyrdom

5. Butter Up

6. Physical Tactic

H. When a frustrated child says or does this...

Pouts or sulks

it's probably...

1. Badgering

2. Temper/Intimidation

3. Threat

4. Martyrdom
5. Butter Up
6. Physical Tactic

I. When a frustrated child says or does this...

"Why?" repeated for the fourth time.

it's probably...

1. Badgering
2. Temper/Intimidation
3. Threat
4. Martyrdom
5. Butter Up
6. Physical Tactic

J. When a frustrated child says or does this...

"I WANT IT NOW!!"

it's probably...

1. Badgering
2. Temper/Intimidation
3. Threat
4. Martyrdom
5. Butter Up
6. Physical Tactic

K. When a frustrated child says or does this...

Goes to his room and slams the door as hard as he can

it's probably...

1. Badgering
2. Temper/Intimidation
3. Threat
4. Martyrdom

5. Butter Up

6. Physical Tactic

L. When a frustrated child says or does this...

"I'm not going to like you anymore!!"

it's probably...

1. Badgering

2. Temper/Intimidation

3. Threat

4. Martyrdom

5. Butter Up

6. Physical Tactic

M. When a frustrated child says or does this...

"You're so mean!"

it's probably...

1. Badgering

2. Temper/Intimidation

3. Threat

4. Martyrdom

5. Butter Up

6. Physical Tactic

N. When a frustrated child says or does this...

Runs out of the house

it's probably...

1. Badgering

2. Temper/Intimidation

3. Threat

4. Martyrdom

5. Butter Up

6. Physical Tactic

O. When a frustrated child says or does this...

"I never get anything."

it's probably...

1. Badgering

2. Temper/Intimidation

3. Threat

4. Martyrdom

5. Butter Up

6. Physical Tactic

The Answers!

A. 3, Threat

B. 2, Temper/Intimidation

C. 1, Badgering

D. 2, Temper/Intimidation

E. 5, Butter Up

F. 4-2, Martyrdom and Intimidation

G. 5-1, Butter Up and Badgering

H. 4, Martyrdom

I. 1, Badgering

J. 2, Intimidation

K. 6, Physical Tactic

L. 3-2 Threat and Intimidation

M. 2, Temper/Intimidation (also possible 4, Martyrdom)

N. 6, Physical Tactic

O. 4, Martyrdom

How well did you do? Remember that if you don't recognize and label testing and manipulation for what it is, you're likely to think something awful or something abnormal is going on. And then your reaction will be off base, and your "management" of the situation runs the risk of being too passive at the one extreme or abusive at the other.

Now see if you can answer this question in regard to each of your children: When my frustrated child says or does this...

Fill in the blank

it's probably...

1. Badgering
2. Temper/Intimidation
3. Threat
4. Martyrdom
5. Butter Up
6. Physical Tactic

What are your kids' favorite testing tactics?

Part IV

What to Do—
The Devil and the
Deep Blue Sea

11

Make Up Your Mind!

S o what have we learned so far? We have learned that parenting has two sides to it, a warm side and a demanding side. The warm side of parenting involves providing food, clothing and shelter to children, having fun with your kids, and giving youngsters emotional support such as affection, praise and sympathetic listening.

The demanding side of parenting involves introducing children to rules, values, limits and character. This side of parenting means that parents do not give their children everything the little ones want, and that adults also expect something from their kids. In other words, adults are charged with the responsibility of teaching their children the critical skill of frustration tolerance. In particular, reasonably demanding adults frustrate kids on a regular basis by doing three things:

1. Asking children to Start doing something that the kids *do not* want to do.
2. Asking children to Stop doing something that the kids *do* want to do.
3. Denying requests from children who want to do something or get something.

Start behavior problems often involve daily routines such as bedtime, eating and homework. Many of these issues come up at the same time everyday. By contrast, Stop behavior problems usually arise consistently but erratically during the day. You know there will be arguing, teasing, yelling, fighting and whining from time to time, but you don't always know the exact times. And finally, like Stop behavior, requests from kids to do something or get something can pop up at any time.

When children are being frustrated in one of these three types of situations, the kids have four choices:

A. Compliance (cooperation)
B. Negotiation (talking things over)
C. Testing and Manipulation (six types plus combinations)
    1. Badgering
    2. Temper/Intimidation
    3. Threat
    4. Martyrdom
    5. Butter Up
    6. Physical Tactics
D. Noncompliance (active or passive)

When adults are acting from their demanding mode, therefore, parents and teachers need to anticipate the situations that will be frustrating for children and then manage these situations effectively in order to minimize testing and noncompliance. When kids are regularly exposed to fair and reasonable discipline, the quality of family life is improved, parents and kids enjoy one another, and children learn healthy self-control.

The demanding side of the parenting equation puts parents between the devil and the deep blue sea. On the one hand, Mom and Dad don't want to give their children everything the youngsters want. On the other hand, Mom and Dad don't relish having to deal with their kids' testing behavior.

Because the four choices of frustrated children are related to one another, kids' testing and manipulation cannot be discussed in isolation. When parental requests (Start and Stop behavior) and the denial of children's requests are bungled by adults, there is a greater risk that kids will skip the alternative of compliance, a greater risk that negotiation will change into testing, and a greater risk that noncompliance will eventually result. Under these circumstances, children do not learn frustration tolerance and self-control. On the other hand, when parents take steps to maximize cooperation, and—when it is appropriate—parents negotiate fairly, testing and noncompliance by children are minimized.

So the problem for adults is: when I am asking a child to Start doing something, Stop doing something, or when I am turning down a child's request, how do I deal with the behavior my frustrated child "chooses" to engage in? In other words, how do I:

    1. Choose a strategy that maximizes compliance? (Chapter 11)
    2. Negotiate or talk reasonably? (Chapter 12)
    3. Manage testing and manipulation? (Chapter 13)
    4. Manage noncompliance? (Chapter 14)

Your first job is to decide what you're going to do. In other words, Make Up Your Mind! Let's look at three examples.

Who's Running the Show?

Let's look at three families in which the parents feel their lives are being run by their children. The first family has a child who is not doing what he's being asked *to do*, the second family has a child who is doing what she's being asked *not to do*, and the third family has a child who has fits whenever a request of his is denied. In short, testing and noncompliance are uncontrolled. Let's examine the trouble first in each situation, then we'll talk about how to fix it. Each example represents one of the typical situations in which parents frustrate children: Start Behavior, Stop Behavior and the denial of children's requests.

Start Behavior: The Case of Picky Pete

Dinnertime at the Jenkins' household is not the pleasant affair it should be. Little Peter, a second grader, doesn't always eat what he's supposed to, and nothing Mom and Dad say seems to have any effect. A typical mealtime scene sounds like this:

"Come on, Peter. Let's get going." (parent request)

"I'm not hungry."

"What did you have to eat after school?"

"Not that much."

"Then how come you're not eating?"

"I am eating!"

"No you're not!"

"We never have anything I like."

Silence. Parents look at each other and continue eating.

"Why do I have to eat this stuff?"

"Because, you know, you want to grow up to be big—strong."

"But I don't like any of it."

"OK, if you don't finish, there will be no dessert and nothing else to eat before bed. Do you understand?"

"Dogfood's better than this junk!"

"Go up to your room, right now, young man! That's no way to talk to anyone!!"

Peter departs.

Interpersonal conflict and eating never mix too well. But at least Peter's parents can suffer in private. This is not the case with our next parent, a single Mom who has to handle her daughter in front of an audience.

Stop Behavior: The Case of Rapid Rita

Rita is four-years-old and loves to go shopping at the grocery store with her Mom. The reason she loves shopping trips is because the store has little kiddie carts she can push around just like her mother does. Rita's Mom, however, does not enjoy shopping with her daughter as much as vice versa. The reason Mom does not like these shopping trips is because, sooner or later, Rita always starts running around with the cart. Last week the little girl ran into the big shopping cart of an older gentleman. Although the man was nice about it and even laughed, Mom is afraid her daughter will hurt someone.

Talk about the devil and the deep blue sea! If Mom doesn't let Rita have a cart, the girl will throw a raging fit—guaranteed—in front of everyone in the store. Mom feels her daughter is running the show.

Mom is correct. Here's how the scene goes when Mom and Rita enter the store:

"Mom! Can I push a cart?"

"I don't think so, dear. Not today. Look at the Fuzzy Bear sign!"

"Why can't I?"

"I just told you, dear. Now please don't start giving me a hard time."

"I wanna push my own one!"

"Now stop that! That's enough! Come on, we've got a lot of things to get."

"I never get to do anything!" Rita starts crying loudly.

"OK, OK! Stop that!" Mom gets a kiddie cart for Rita. Rita grabs the cart, but Mom holds the cart for a second and looks at her daughter firmly.

"Rita, look at me. You have to promise me you won't run with the cart. You might hurt someone. Do you understand me?"

"Yes."

"And you promise you won't run with the cart?"

"Yes."

"Say I promise."

"I promise."

"OK. Now let's get our stuff. I'll put some things in your cart."

Rita does just fine for six minutes. Then she starts running with her kiddie cart, giggling as she zooms along past the spaghetti sauce. Her mother pretends she doesn't notice, then she cuts the shopping trip short after getting only one-third of the things she needed. Maybe she can come back later and get the rest of what she wants by herself.

Denial of a Child's Request: The Case of Moody Matthew

Matthew never likes to take "No" for an answer. His parents feel a sense of dread whenever he asks for something or asks to do something. Matt's parents say that their son has raised pouting to a new art form. Here's how:

"Mom, can I go to Bobby's?"

"No, dear, it's too late."

"But he's got that neat new game he wants to show me."

"Not tonight, Matthew. You can go tomorrow."

"Oh come on. Why can't I? It's just across the street."

"I know where Bobby lives."

"I never get to do anything!"

"You never get to do anything? Remember Sunday—two days ago? Was that what you call not doing anything?"

"You let Marci go to Kristen's."

"She went right after school. Now it's already past 7:30."

"I promise I'll be back in ten minutes."

"It will be too late by then. There's this thing called shower and then bedtime, remember?"

"This is stupid! I'm not taking any dumb shower!"

"Don't start yelling at me, young man! Why do we have to go through this all the time!?"

Matthew is silent. He crosses the room and lies down on the couch, where his mother can easily see him. Folding his arms forcefully, he lies there sulking and staring at the ceiling. Mom hates it when he does this. Why does he have to make a federal case out of everything? Mom goes over and crouches down by the couch.

"Listen. Don't we love you? Don't we do a lot for you? Don't we give you most of the things you want?"

"Yeah."

"Then why can't you do just this one little thing for us? Just for tonight. Huh?"

"I don't know."

Pause.

"Listen, I'll let you go over there, but only for ONE HALF HOUR. Then you have to come back without me calling you. Do you understand?"

"Yeah!" A now-excited Matt hops off the couch and is out the door in a flash.

Forty-five minutes later, Mom calls to Bobby's house across the street and asks her son to come home.

What *To* Do: Make Up Your Mind!

The first step in managing testing and manipulation is to try to prevent it by getting kids to cooperate. And the first step in getting kids to cooperate is to have a plan. When problems like those in the three families we just described are occurring, Moms and Dads need to take a moment (or sometimes longer) to stop and think. That involves the following:

1. **Label the problem behavior.**
2. **Identify what is not working.**
3. **Change your thinking from wishful to realistic.**
4. **Choose or Restructure.**
5. **Anticipate your child's reactions.**

Let's apply these steps to the Cases of Picky Peter, Rapid Rita and Moody Matthew.

1. Picky Peter: Label the problem behavior

Parent/child conflicts usually occur in situations where a parent is asking a child to Start doing something (go to bed, do homework, get out of bed, eat dinner), Stop doing something (arguing, whining, fighting, tantruming, yelling), or situations in which a parent is not granting a child's request (no candy now, can't sleep over, can't ride the roller coaster). The presence of a parent request or a child request, therefore, is a cue that it's time to start thinking!

Most nights Peter is having trouble finishing his dinner. Eating a meal is a Start Behavior—something you want children *to* do. As we have seen before, Start Behavior problems involve passive noncompliance. Since Start behavior often takes time (eating can take more than a half hour, for example), extra motivational strategies are sometimes required. Is this parental request important? Certainly. Eating is important, so Mom and Dad do not need time to think over the importance of eating or to negotiate mealtime every night with their son.

Peter's problem also involves testing and manipulation:

"We never have anything I like."
Martyrdom
"Why do I have to eat this stuff?"
Badgering
"But I don't like any of it."
Badgering
"Dogfood's better than this junk!"
Temper/Intimidation

Peter's testing and manipulation is aggravated by the fact that his parents are not handling the situation well. Instead of thinking, "What is *your* problem!!", Peter's mother and father need to think, "What is *the* problem?"

2. Picky Peter: Identify what is not working

Any psychologist, psychiatrist, social worker or counselor who works with children knows that one of the biggest problems you run into is impulsive behavior. Impulsive children act without thinking; they have a tendency to act out whatever impulse they are feeling at the moment—without regard to the consequences. Impulsive kids blurt out comments in the classroom and interrupt other people's conversations. They may also hit, yell, lie or steal, then worry about the fallout later. Another way of looking at this problem is the notion we have repeatedly discussed: impulsive children suffer from *low frustration tolerance*.

Everyone has heard the famous line, "Full speed ahead—damn the torpedoes!" For impulsive kids the line is simply, "Full speed ahead!" When they act, these kids aren't aware that there are any torpedoes. Research shows clearly that due to their lack of foresight, as impulsive children become adults, they suffer tremendously themselves and also present big problems to others. These individuals are simply less successful in life. They have lower incomes, more trouble establishing and keeping relationships, more trouble with smoking and drinking, more trouble with the law, more trouble driving. Their list of problems is a long one.

It is clear, then, that impulsive, acting-without-thinking behavior isn't very healthy for anyone. It usually works better to think things over a bit—or sometimes a lot—before acting. That's what our brains are for.

The problem we are concerned about here is impulsive parenting. It's an epidemic. Even adults who generally handle life reasonably well have a strong tendency to shoot from the hip when it comes to parenting. These Moms and Dads simply react with the first thing that comes to their minds. And when kids are talking, testing or being defiant, impulsive responses from adults usually don't work very well.

With Picky Pete, for example, Mom and Dad's motivational efforts consisted of the following:

> *"Come on, Peter. Let's get going."*
> Simple request
> *"What did you have to eat after school?"*
> Question
> *"Then how come you're not eating?"*
> Question, nagging
> *"No you're not!"*
> Nagging
> *"Because, you know, you want to grow up to be big—strong."*
> Reasoning
> *"OK, if you don't finish, there will be no dessert and nothing else to eat before bed. Do you understand?"*
> Threat, appeal to reason

So what's not working? A simple request, questions (designed to "get to the bottom of the problem"), nagging, reasoning and threat. This whole package is a good example of impulsive—and slightly desperate—parenting. Learning to think first before responding to your frustrated children takes some effort in the beginning, but it often becomes second nature after a short time.

Another important-and-unfortunate mistake Peter's parents made was to reinforce the testing and manipulation tactics of their son. They did this by giving Peter his way: He got to leave the table and not finish his dinner. (Whether or not you agree with the philosophy of these parents regarding eating is not the point.) To not have to eat what he didn't want to eat was Peter's original objective, and his Martyrdom, Badgering and Temper achieved that goal for him. Peter will be automatically conditioned to remember that his tactics were successful, so the boy will be even harder to manage the next time around. And the well-being of this family was sacrificed along the way.

3. Picky Peter: Change your thinking from wishful to realistic

Mom and Dad have put no thought into managing the problem of Peter's eating because they simply expect that he should eat. Many kids do eat with no problem at all; but this kid doesn't. Peter is a member of the Picky Eaters Club. After their son didn't eat well on Tuesday, however, his parents will nevertheless expect that he'll eat well on Wednesday. Mr. and Mrs. Jenkins expected their last trip to Hawaii to be perfect, too.

To turn things around Mom and Dad need to start expecting that Peter will continue to be a picky eater. He was probably born that way. Perhaps his taste-bud genes came from another planet. But one thing is sure: Dinnertime battles over Peter's eating will only make his pickiness worse.

When Peter is not around, his parents say to each other "What's the matter with this kid?", "Why does he have to get so belligerent and rude?", and "What are we doing wrong?"

"What's the matter with this kid?" Probably nothing very serious. He doesn't eat a lot. "Why does he have to get so belligerent and rude?" He doesn't have to be, but the longer useless conversations about eating go on, the worse Peter gets. His responses are just good, old-fashioned testing and manipulation, rather than indications that he needs psychological help. "What are we doing wrong?" Mom and Dad did not cause their son to dislike a lot of foods, and neither Mom nor Dad is a bad cook. But Peter's parents are handling the situation poorly, which helps to make their son's testing worse.

4. Picky Peter: Choose or Restructure

Sometimes managing your youngsters simply means deciding what you are going to do right this minute and choosing from a list of reasonable alternatives. Do I insist that my child follow my directions at this moment? Do I give her what she wants right now or not?

Other times, however, at the moment that a conflict is occurring, parents' efforts are hampered because the adults are not aware of what the good alternatives might be. *It's amazing how perfectly reasonable adults often repeat, over and over, parenting tactics that don't work!* "Every night we go through the same thing!" usually means "Every night we nag, argue and scream at our son when he doesn't do what we expect." "We've tried everything and nothing works with this child!" usually means "We've done nothing consistently." A basic law of human nature dictates that exasperation makes people less creative rather than more creative. Frustrated Moms and Dads get into ruts.

When parents find themselves making statements like these, it's time to go back to the drawing boards and design a different approach to the problem. Actually, many mothers and fathers have been so hurried and so busy for so long that they've never really sat down at the parental drawing board in the first place. In other words, busy schedules, make for impulsive parenting.

So Peter's Mom and Dad decide that they will not let things go on as they have been. They simply won't allow their family life to be miserable. *Anything* would be better than the dinnertime conflicts they have been experiencing. Sometimes restructuring a situation with conflict potential involves just a few minor adjustments. One thought Peter's mother and father had, for example, was to simply limit Peter's after-school and after-dinner snacking, and then just let him eat whatever he wanted to at dinner. Even that minor change, they thought, would be an improvement.

Other times, however, designing a different approach can amount to a complete overhaul. That's what Peter's parents do—they eventually decided to change a lot of things. There will be several parts to their new strategy: (1) new rule: Peter cannot eat any snacks after 4:15, (2) Peter will be given smaller portions, (3) within 45 minutes Peter must finish three of four food offerings per meal and at least taste the one he doesn't choose to finish, and (4) getting dessert will depend upon the above. Mom and Dad will repeat these rules once before each meal for the first week, then they will keep quiet. Peter's parents also agree not to nag their son during the meal, but they will discuss their plan with him before starting.

Notice that these parents used several basic principles that are frequently useful in designing possible solutions:

1. They began by accepting Peter the way he was, not by how they wished he'd be.
2. They decided to talk less (and get less excited) themselves.
3. They gave their son some choice in the matter.
4. They used rewards and consequences.

5. Picky Peter: Anticipate your child's reactions

The final step, before trying out anything new, is to troubleshoot in advance the new solution. Which of the four choices of frustrated children will Peter pick? Will fresh ideas eliminate the problems and the frustration altogether? If the child's choice is cooperation, fine. But what if his choice is testing and manipulation? Which tactic will he most likely turn to? Will Mom and Dad be able to understand that frustrated children test their parents sometimes, or will they view testing as an unpardonable sin?

Worse yet, could noncompliance become an issue? Is this child capable of doing what his parents don't want him to do in this situation, and would he consider doing that? What if Peter eats snacks after 4:15, doesn't finish three courses, or sneaks a forbidden dessert afterwards? No wishful thinking is allowed; it's essential to be ready for anything!

After redesigning their dinnertime strategy, Peter's mother and father are hopeful but cautious. They think they may be on to something good, but they are also wary that they may have to again face their son's testing and passive noncompliance.

The Case of Rapid Rita

Let's try out our Make Up Your Mind! format with our speedy, four-year-old cart pusher.

1. Rapid Rita: Label the problem behavior

The problem with Rita involves both noncompliance and testing. Rita is doing what her mother doesn't want her to do: run in the store with the little shopping cart. This is a Stop behavior—something this parent wants this child to cease doing. Running with the cart is also an example of active noncompliance, but the active noncompliance is less worrisome in this case because Rita is only four. It is very likely that the little girl gets excited and simply forgets her mother's instructions—no matter how clear and definite Mom tries to be beforehand.

The difficulty with this child also involves testing and manipulation, which is triggered by Mom's denial of the girl's request to have the cart. Rita wants that cart, and by hook or by crook, she's going to get it! Her testing tactics included the following:

> *"Why can't I?"*
> Badgering
> *"I wanna push my own one!"*
> Badgering, Temper
> *"I never get to do anything!" Rita starts crying loudly.*
> Martyrdom, Temper
> *"I promise."*
> Butter Up—not unsolicited, however!

Like Peter's testing and manipulation, Rita's testing is also aggravated by the fact that her mother doesn't quite know what to do. Mom's denial of her daughter's request was ambivalent and weak, so Rita went straight for the jugular. Then Mom made a bad move worse, reinforcing her daughter's testing by letting her have the kiddie cart.

2. Rapid Rita: Identify what is not working

Mom tried everything but throwing in the kitchen sink. Nothing seemed to work. Mom's strategies included:

> *"I don't think so, dear. Not today. Look at the Fuzzy Bear sign!"*
> Weak and ambivalent denial of the request, attempt at distraction
> *"I just told you, dear. Now please don't start giving me a hard time."*
> Repeat request, begging
> *"Now stop that! That's enough! Come on, we've got a lot of things to get."*
> Angry demand, distraction

"OK, OK! Stop that!" Mom gets a kiddie cart for Rita.
Capitulation
*"Rita, look at me. You have to promise me you won't run with
the cart. You might hurt someone. Do you understand me?"*
Reasoning, explanation
"And you promise you won't run with the cart?"
Asking child to verbalize commitment
"Say I promise."
Again asking child to verbalize commitment

The only way Mom found to end the testing and manipulation was
capitulation. Giving a frustrated child what he wants ends testing, but
giving in always makes it harder in the future for parents to set limits.
Unfortunately, this mother's capitulation did not solve the problem of
noncompliance; her daughter still wound up running with the cart.

3. Rapid Rita: Change your thinking from wishful to realitistic

Mom has had difficulty facing this problem with her daughter because she
keeps hoping that the child will simply behave some day. Maybe Rita will
lose interest in the cart. Maybe she will magically stop having fits when
Mom suggests she can't have a cart. Or maybe Rita will stop getting
excited and running around the store.

To turn things around Mom needs to start expecting that Rita will
continue to want the cart, will continue to throw a fit if she doesn't get it,
and will continue to run with the cart in the store. Somewhere in the
sequence Mom will have to draw the line.

This mother is a single parent, which makes it harder for her to go to
the store by herself. When Rita's Mom talks to Rita's grandmother, she
says things like "Why can't she just take 'No' for an answer?" and "I can't
stand another shopping trip—she's going to drive me crazy!"

"Why can't she just take 'No' for an answer?" Because Rita's only
four and she really wants that kiddie cart. Even grocery stores have a
perverse ability to understand what turns kids on. "I can't stand another
shopping trip—she's going to drive me crazy!" Yes, this situation is very
aggravating, but it's not the end of the world. Rita's probably not going to

kill anyone, but she is in need of a lesson in frustration tolerance. Right now all the little girl is learning is how to be aggressive and how to push other people around. Mom needs to come up with a solution soon.

4. Rapid Rita: Choose or restructure

In the course of a conversation with a sympathetic friend, Rita's mother considers several alternatives. Mom really doesn't want to go through another one of those awful scenes. She doesn't like being embarrassed in public, but she also doesn't want to ruin her relationship with her daughter. Mom has the foresight to appreciate the fact that if situations like this become chronic, she and Rita will wind up simply not liking each other.

One thought is to not take daughter along when Mom goes shopping. There are two problems with this idea, however. Being a single parent, this mother doesn't have a lot of backup. And she does not want to be imposing on her friends all the time. The other thing, though, is that Mom and Rita used to enjoy shopping together—before the advent of the kiddie carts. Rita used to ride in the cart, or walk along side, and everything was fine.

So Rita's mother makes two decisions. First of all, Mom is going to continue to take her daughter with her shopping. Going together is more convenient and Mom wants it to be fun again. Second, Mom will not let her daughter have a small cart, because the little girl is just too young to be able to not run with it. Mom is determined, but there will be one big bridge to cross before the good old days return.

That big bridge will be entering the store and Rita's request for a kiddie cart. Mom decides that she will warn her daughter once as they are parking that the girl won't be getting a cart. Mom, however, knows that will not be the end of it. So as they enter the store, Mom will give one— and only one— firm "No" to her daughter, she will say nothing else, and she will take a big shopping cart and keep moving.

5. Rapid Rita: Anticipate your child's reactions

Rita's Mom gets all the "Wouldn't it be nice if's..." out of her head and realistically anticipates that her offspring will go nuclear when she can't get her cart. Then, Mom figures, the little girl will most likely follow her through the store while continuing to scream at the top of her lungs

(Temper) and continuing to repeat her demand over and over (Badgering). But Mom also believes that her daughter will eventually quiet down (it may take a few shopping trips), forget the whole thing, and once again enjoy shopping with her Mom.

Mom makes her plan and takes a deep breath.

The Case of Moody Matthew

Now let's apply our five Make Up Your Mind! steps to the martyr-like Matthew. Matt wanted to go over to a friend's house, but his mother thought it was too late.

1. Moody Matthew: Label the problem behavior

The problem here involves the denial of a child's request (going to his friend's house). As with our other examples, Matthew is also heavily into testing and manipulation. He knows his parents have trouble setting limits, so whenever he thinks they have left the door open a crack, he goes for the gold. His tactics include the following:

"But he's got that neat new game he wants to show me."
Badgering
"Oh come on. Why can't I? It's just across the street."
Badgering
"I never get to do anything!"
Martyrdom
"You let Marci go to Kristen's."
Badgering, hint of Martyrdom
"I promise I'll be back in ten minutes."
Butter up
"This is stupid! I'm not taking any dumb shower!"
Temper/Intimidation, Threat
Matthew is silent. He crosses the room and lies down on the couch, where his mother can easily see him. Folding his arms forcefully, he lies there sulking and staring at the ceiling.
Martyrdom

The only testing method Matthew didn't use, thank heaven, was engaging in some Physical Tactic.

2. Moody Matthew: Identify what is not working

Like her son, Matthew's Mom also used a variety of tactics. In fact, the use of multiple tactics is often a sure sign that the user—whether parent or child—is not getting what he or she wants and is still fishing around for a successful approach. Mom's "strategies" involved impulsive parenting, rather than reflections of any well-thought-out plan. Mom's reactions to her son included:

> *"No, dear, it's too late."*
Clear denial of the request with brief explanation
> *"Not tonight, Matthew. You can go tomorrow."*
Repeating the denial of the request
> *"I know where Bobby lives."*
Pretend information giving—Mom's getting sidetracked a bit
> *"You never get to do anything? Remember Sunday—two days ago? Was that what you call not doing anything?"*
Pretend reasoning—Mom's really sidetracked now
> *"She went right after school. Now it's already past 7:30."*
Pretend reasoning—giving more irrelevant information
> *"It will be too late by then. There's this thing called shower and then bedtime, remember?"*
Repeating the denial of the request, reasoning
> *"Don't start yelling at me, young man! Why do we have to go through this all the time!?"*
New command, desperate-but-ineffective question regarding her son's testing
> *"Listen. Don't we love you? Don't we do a lot for you? Don't we give you most of the things you want?"*
Guilt induction
> *"Then why can't you do just this one little thing for us? Huh?"*
Guilt induction
> *"Listen, I'll let you go over there, but only for ONE HALF HOUR.*

Then you have to come back without me calling you. Do you
understand?"
Very thinly disguised capitulation, followed by weak face-saving
attempt at firmness and reason

Mom started out very well with a clear denial of her son's request.
There was also nothing wrong with repeating that denial. But one
repetition is enough. Next, however—in the face of her son's persistent
testing—Mom's approach disintegrates, going from pretend reasoning
(as if this information were going to make any difference!) to repeating
herself to attempts at guilt induction. In the end, though, it's Matthew's
guilt induction tactic, not Mom's, that wins the day, as this parent once
again caves in.

3. Moody Matthew: Change your thinking from wishful to realistic

Matthew's problem is the traditional "Not being able to take 'No' for an
answer." What's the matter with this kid? Most likely there is nothing
especially wrong with Matthew. In fact, if you asked his parents at a time
when no conflict was occurring, they'd honestly say that their son was
"basically a good kid." Like most children, though, he gets frustrated
when he doesn't get what he wants and he's inclined toward testing and
manipulation when he doesn't get a good parental "No." He will probably
be a lot less pushy and a lot less disrespectful once his parents learn how
to effectively draw the line with him.

4. Moody Matthew: Choose or redesign

Matthew's parents decide that they will not allow unpleasant conflicts
over denied requests to go on any longer. They will not, however, resort
to "Rambo" parenting—attemps at overkill that involve parental tantrums
based on the philosophy that "All this kid needs is a good... etc., etc."
Regarding situations that involve the denial of their child's requests,
Matthew's parents decide (1) they will respectfully listen first to any
request their son makes, (2) they will then take time to think the request
over, if necessary, and (3) they will give their son a clear response—once;

after that they will no longer talk. This system will also be discussed with Matthew before it is started, and his input will be encouraged.

5. Moody Matthew: Anticipate your child's reactions

Mom and Dad cross their fingers. At this point these parents are not hopeful that there will be an easy solution, but they are ready to keep tuning up their plan until something better is found. If Matthew cooperates, that will be wonderful. His parents will have made it clear what he can talk over and what he cannot. And they will do their best to not continue making useless verbal responses to his testing and manipulation when it occurs.

So the parents in our three families have redesigned their approaches to their problem situations. ow it's time for them to actually run some clinical trials! How will it go in each family? How will the kids respond? We'll find out in the next chapter. A lot will depend upon an often overlooked and much misunderstood part of parenting and discipline: talking.

12

Stop Talking!

K nowing how and when to talk is a frequently misinterpreted parenting skill, because most people these days still assume the more communication, the better. Nothing could be further from the truth.

Clinical Trial: The Case of Picky Pete

Dad explains the New Deal to his son: If Peter eats three out of four items on his plate, the boy can have his dessert. The serving sizes will be smaller and Peter has to at least taste the one he doesn't choose to eat. The first meal under the new regime goes well. Even though they are a bit nervous, both parents avoid any anxious prompting. Peter finishes his smaller portions of pork, mashed potatoes and peas, but he forgoes the salad. He gets ice cream for dessert.

Good compliance, no testing and manipulation.

After the mealtime overhaul, the first week passes without any unpleasant incidents. Peter and his parents actually enjoy one another's company; the dinner table conversation is spirited and friendly.

"Pete, how was that movie you saw with your friend?"

"Oh, cool! You guys gotta see it!"

"You really think we'd like it at our advanced ages?"

"Oh, yeah! Let's go—I'll go see it again."

"Well, if your mother's willing, it might be possible."

"Mom, you gotta go. It's so neat! There's this one part where..."

Trouble comes, though, the following Thursday, when the dinner selection is barbecued chicken, broccoli, salad and noodles. Peter eats the chicken and the noodles, but declines the other two items.

"I'm done."

"You only finished two things."

"Well these others taste funny."

"They don't taste funny to me. Just try them for once."

"I don't like this stuff. It makes my stomach queasy."

"Now don't start making up excuses. I'm sure your stomach is going to be just fine."

"It's not an excuse! I said I'm done."

"OK, but the deal is no dessert. We have ice cream bars tonight."

"Aw, come on. That's not fair!"

"You hardly ate anything! What *is* your problem!?"

"I'll eat more chicken and noodles."

"That's not the deal."

"Well this 'new deal thing' is really stupid! All my friends think you guys are weird. No one else I know has a big plan for how they eat their dinner."

"Sorry, but we don't have time to worry about your friends. The person we do have to worry about is you. Now we weren't put on this planet to torture you constantly, which is what you seem to think. All we want is for you to be healthy by eating what you're supposed to, and if you want, we can all sit here and wait for you til the cows come home!"

What's happening here? Plenty of "communication," that's for sure! But in the process a perfectly good deal is getting blown apart because these parents forgot to stop talking. *Parents who talk too much immunize their children against listening.*

Two-way Communication

Let's step aside for a minute and examine the slippery problem that just threw Peter's parents for a loop: talking.

Human communication is a fascinating subject. Communication and language help accomplish amazing feats. People talk to one another to have fun, to feel a sense of belonging, to exchange information and to get jobs done.

"Did you hear the one about the guy...?"
"What a day I've had!"
"What's the balance on that checking account?"
"You bring the rakes and I'll bring the leaf bags."

Though talking with other human beings can be a source of great enjoyment and can solve a lot of problems, the exact opposite can also be true: Talking can be the mediator of great conflict. Therefore it's important, when we're discussing kids' testing and manipulation, to clarify some things about human communication. Parents not only need to know what to say, they also need to know when it's time to talk. Ironically perhaps, when it comes to managing testing, the most important communication skill for Mom and Dad to learn is knowing when to keep quiet.

Here's the problem: Most people think of talking as a two-way information exchange. They assume that if two people are talking back and forth to each other, there must be a two-way information exchange going on. Very often, of course, that's exactly what is happening:

"Do you want to go to the game today?"
"Sounds good! What time does it start?"
"1:30 p.m. I can pick you up."
"OK. How much are the tickets?"
"Never mind. It's on me. It's your birthday."
"Well, thank you!"

This was a nice, brief two-way information exchange. Two individuals pass some information back and forth about what they want or don't want to do, and then they decide what is going to be done. The discussion is logical and reasonable—and friendly as well.

That's how it was earlier with one of our Kathy and Dad episodes.

"Kathy, it's time to get ready for bed."
"Dad, can I stay up for just fifteen more minutes? I want to finish
   this game. I'll even take a bath if you let me."
"OK, young lady, but I'm holding you to it. Bath time is in fifteen
   minutes sharp!"
"Thanks, Dad!"

Dad starts things off by giving his daughter some information: It's time for bed. Not liking this idea, Kathy chooses the second option of frustrated kids: Negotiation. She gives two pieces of new information back to her father: I don't want to go to bed right now and I'll take a bath if you let me stay up for fifteen more minutes. Though he knows he has to be careful with negotiating daily routines, on this night Dad buys into the Negotiation idea. He gives new information back to his daughter: OK, I'll change the rule for tonight, but no more than 15 minutes. The brief bargaining session is concluded. The talk was reasonable and the conclusion satisfactory for both people.

When Talking Is Not Talking

When parents are acting from the demanding side of their parenting job, denying requests from their kids or making requests of their kids, talking can often become trickier. Remember Difficult Kathy and Gentle Dad?

Gentle Dad: "Kathy, it's time to get ready for bed."
Difficult Kathy: "Ah, come on. Just a few more minutes."
Gentle Dad: "Not tonight, honey. You've got a big day tomorrow."
Difficult Kathy: "Just twenty minutes."
Gentle Dad: "Listen, dear, you really are going to need some sleep."
Difficult Kathy: "I was just starting to have fun. Now I have to stop.
   I never get to do anything around here!"
Gentle Dad: "OK, but just twenty minutes. Then you promise me
   you won't give me a hard time?"
Difficult Kathy: "OK."

Dad again starts things off by giving his daughter some information: It's time for bed. Kathy gives new information back to her father: I don't want to go right now. Looks like a two-way exchange, right? So far it is, but from this point in the conversation, this particular dialogue ceases to be a genuine information exchange based upon reason. Instead, it becomes an emotional struggle to see who's going to get his or her way. Kathy is testing and Dad is on the defensive. The conversation really boils down to nothing more than this:

Gentle Dad: "Kathy, it's time to get ready for bed."
Difficult Kathy: "I don't want to."
Gentle Dad: "You have to."
Difficult Kathy: "I don't want to!"
Gentle Dad: "You really should."
Difficult Kathy: "I REALLY don't want to!!"
Gentle Dad: "I give up."
Difficult Kathy: "Good."

You might argue about exactly where the conversation stopped being a real information exchange, but you have to admit that it soon became only a battle of wills. In this example, Difficult Kathy's personality easily overcame her Dad's easygoing temperament. Kathy was willing to fight, if necessary, and Dad was not.

What Kathy and her father were having was a *pretend* conversation. The noises coming from the mouths of this child and this parent really were nothing more than an emotional war. It was all about emotion, and all about winning and losing. The content of the words was irrelevant. When "talks" like these are allowed to go on, testing and manipulation from children get worse and the chances of noncompliance increase.

Pretend conversations have the following characteristics:

1. The conversation starts out *information-based*, but it soon becomes *emotion-based*.
2. The *longer* the conversation goes on, the *worse* the conflict gets.
3. The longer the conversation goes on, the *less the likelihood of a satisfactory resolution.*

4. The "winner" (the one who gets his or her way) of the
interaction will not be the one who makes the most sense, it
will be *the person who is more able to successfully
use emotional clout* to get the "opponent" to give in.

Difficult Kathy and Difficult Dad provided us with a more extreme
example of a pretend conversation:

Difficult Dad: "Kathy, time for bed."
Difficult Kathy: "Just a few more minutes."
Difficult Dad: "I said now!"
Difficult Kathy: "I'm right in the middle of this program!"
Difficult Dad: "You gonna move or am I gonna have to do it
  for you!?"
Difficult Kathy: "FOR CRYING OUT LOUD WHY CAN'T I
  EVER DO ANYTHING I WANT TO AROUND HERE!"
(Starts to get up.)
Difficult Dad: "YOU KNOW SOMETHING? I'M SICK AND
  TIRED OF YOUR COMPLAINING ABOUT EVERY
  LITTLE THING YOU'RE ASKED TO DO."
(Also starts to get up.)
Difficult Kathy: "OH SHUT UP! WHY DO YOU HAVE TO
  SCREAM AT ME ALL THE TIME!!"
Difficult Dad: "YOU WATCH THAT MOUTH OF YOURS,
  YOUNG LADY! I WOULDN'T HAVE TO RAISE MY VOICE
  IF YOU'D DO WHAT YOU'RE TOLD ONCE IN A MILLION
  YEARS!!"
Difficult Kathy: "Living in this house SUCKS! TOTALLY SUCKS!
  I wish I were dead!" (Heads off to her room.)
Difficult Dad: "GET UP THERE! NOW!!"

In this example, neither Kathy nor her father show any great aversion
to getting into a fight. Since the real content of the words has become
immaterial, the translation of what these two people are really saying to
one another is something like this:

Difficult Dad: "Kathy, time for bed."

Difficult Kathy: "Just a few more minutes."

Difficult Dad: "You have to go to bed."

Difficult Kathy: "I don't want to go to bed."

Difficult Dad:"You have to!"

Difficult Kathy: "I DON'T WANT TO!" (Starts to get up.)

Difficult Dad: "YOU HAVE TO!!" (Also starts to get up.)

Difficult Kathy: "I DON'T WANT TO!!"

Difficult Dad: "YOU HAVE TO!!!"

Difficult Kathy: "I GIVE UP!!"

Difficult Dad: "It's about time!"

Information exchange? Negotiation? Not quite. Logic has departed and this "conversation" is based simply upon the emotional clout of the two contestants. The odd thing, however, is that on the surface it appears as though Kathy and her Dad are still trying to give new information to each other so they can solve the problem. But the two are only pretending to exchange information. Based on the content of the words alone—minus all the emotion—it's as if these two are saying something absurd like this:

Difficult Dad: "Would it help, dear, if I escorted you to your room?"

Difficult Kathy: "No, Dad. But you know, I truly feel I don't get to do what I want often enough. So let's do it my way."

Difficult Dad: "But you know, honey, you do do a lot of complaining. So let's do it my way."

Difficult Kathy: "But father, it really isn't right for you to raise your voice to me. So let's do it my way."

Difficult Dad:"I belive you're incorrect, darling. You are more often disrespectful to me. So let's do it my way."

Difficult Kathy: "OK, I'll go, but this is extremely disappointing to me. And you should be aware that I really don't enjoy living in this particular family."

Picky Pete, Rapid Rita and Moody Matthew

Pretend conversations make a parent's job difficult, because these dialogues are confusing. Often you get caught up in the give-and-take before you realize what's happening. Then you are presented with a quandry: What's the best way to manage a pretend conversation? Do I respond to the content of the words, the emotion or both?

We saw pretend conversations before in our three examples of family conflict:

Picky Pete

"Then how come you're not eating?"

"I am eating!"

"No you're not!"

"We never have anything I like." (Martyrdom)

Silence. Parents look at each other and continue eating.

"Why do I have to eat this stuff?" (Badgering)

"Because, you know, you want to grow up to be big—strong."

"But I don't like any of it." (Martyrdom)

"OK, if you don't finish, there will be no dessert and nothing else to eat before bed. Do you understand?"

Rapid Rita

"Why can't I?" (Badgering)

"I just told you, dear. Now please don't start giving me a hard time."

"I wanna push my own one!" (Badgering, Temper)

"Now stop that! That's enough! Come on, we've got a lot of things to get."

"I never get to do anything!" Rita starts crying loudly. (Martyrdom)

Moody Matthew

"Oh come on. Why can't I? It's just across the street." (Badgering)

"I know where Bobby lives."

"I never get to do anything!" (Martyrdom)

"You never get to do anything? Remember Sunday—two days ago? Was that what you call not doing anything?"

"You let Marci go to Kristen's." (Badgering)

"She finished her homework. You were goofing around."

"I promise I'll do it when I get back." (Butter up)

So when you have a pretend conversation going on, what do you do? Do you respond to the content of the words, to the emotion or to both? The answer is None of the Above. By the time a pretend dialogue is occurring, the situation has become ridiculous—the horse has already left the barn. What parents need to do must be done a lot earlier: Draw the line and be quiet. Here's how:

How and When to Talk

When parents are faced with conflict conversations like those above, for some reason they have an awful time accepting the obvious: Talking is not working! *News flash!! More Talking Doesn't Always Help!!* More talking only makes matters worse. Oh my goodness, the world is falling apart! What do I do if I can't talk? All those parenting books said...

Relax, the situation is not really that desperate. Here's what needs to be done:

> **1. Should we negotiate?**
> **2. State your case.**
> **3. Stop talking.**
> **4. Let your child decide what to do.**
> **5. Respond to your child's choice.**

Let's apply these steps to the Case of Picky Peter. Recall that Peter's parents had designed a new solution to his dinner time problem. The plan had gone well until it ran full-tilt into broccoli and salad.

"I'm done."

"You only finished two things."

"Well these others taste funny."

"They don't taste funny to me. Just try them for once."

"I don't like this stuff. It makes my stomach queasy."

"Now don't start making up excuses. I'm sure your stomach is going to be just fine."

"It's not an excuse! I said I'm done."

"OK, but the deal is no dessert. We have ice cream bars tonight."

"Aw, come on. That's not fair!"

"You didn't hardly eat anything! What *is* your problem!?"

"I'll eat more chicken and noodles."

"That's not the deal."

"Well this 'new deal thing' is really stupid! All my friends think you guys are weird. No one else I know has a big plan for how they eat their dinner."

"Sorry, but we don't have time to worry about your friends. The person we do have to worry about is you. Now we weren't put on this planet to torture you constantly, which is what you seem to think. All we want is for you to be healthy by eating what you're supposed to, and if you want, we can all sit here and wait for you till the cows come home!"

1. Picky Peter: Should we negotiate?

Too often we parents start trying to manage a situation or talk to a frustrated child before we have really decided what we want to do. When children sense this uncertainty in their mothers and fathers, the kids usually test and manipulate more. Before moving ahead in managing a specific situation, parents need to ask themselves several questions. One of the most important questions is: Do I need time to think it over?

If you do need time to think over a child's request, it is sometimes also a good idea to talk it over with your youngster. In other words, Negotiation is a legitimate option. When your daughter, for example, asks if you can take her to the show, your response might be "Give me fifteen minutes to think it over" or "Tell me what you've got in mind."

In our last scene, the mistake Peter's parents make is getting sidetracked and overlooking the fact that they had already made up their minds. They had a deal that covered this situation: If Peter only eats two items, he doesn't get his dessert. That's it; he's not going to die because he declined either salad or broccoli on this particular night. But there is no need to renegotiate the deal right this moment at the dinner table.

Peter, however, first gets his parents a little off balance when he says:

"Well these others (salad and broccoli) taste funny."

"I don't like this stuff. It makes my stomach queasy."

Mom and Dad get somewhat irritated by these comments. They're a little insulted and they think their son's making excuses. This increased level of emotion in Peter's parents begins to produce cognitive regression and forgetfulness; Mom and Dad start falling into their old rut. Peter then knocks his parents totally off base when he says:

"Aw, come on. That's not fair!"

This crystal clear example of Badgering and Martyrdom is not recognized as testing and manipulation by the adults at the table. Instead, Mom and Dad continue with what is now a pretend conversation, and everybody winds up getting really mad:

"Well this 'new deal thing' is really stupid!"
"We can all sit here and wait for you till the cows come home!"

Let's do this scene over, and let's imagine that this time Mom and Dad *do remember* that they have already made up their minds and should not renegotiate. They already have a deal and, in fact, it is working well. What these parents really need to do next, therefore, is to state their case.

2. Picky Peter: State your case

When parents are making demands of their children or denying children's requests, the adults need to be *clear, firm and brief* when stating their case. Clear: No wishy-washy phrases, questions ("Don't you think it's time for bed?"), or revolting "we" language ("Shouldn't we be starting our homework?"). Firm: If you have made up your mind, but you still feel a little funny about what you've decided, keep your funny feelings out of your voice. Brief: Extra talking and extra emotion (often anxiety) on your part simply lets your youngsters know (1) that you are afraid of what they are going to do and (2) that you are not ready for them.

Here's how Peter's parents might state their case to their son:

"I'm done."
"You only finished two things."
"Well these others taste funny."
"OK, but the deal is no dessert. We have ice cream bars tonight."

"Aw, come on. That's not fair!"

"That's our deal."

"I'll eat more chicken and noodles."

Silence.

"Well this 'new deal thing' is really stupid!"

Silence.

Grumbling to himself, Peter leaves the table.

Most excellent response on the part of Mom and Dad. A+! In one fell swoop, Mom and Dad also accomplished the next three steps on our what-to-do list:

3. Stop talking.
4. Let your child decide what to do.
5. Respond to your child's choice.

3. Picky Peter: Stop Talking

Peter's parents stopped all the pretend talking. No more useless attempts at a fake "information exchange" that is meaningless because the conversation is really all about emotion and winning vs. losing. They also stopped pretending that they were going to give their son three reasons why he should do what they wanted, and that he would then say "Gee, I never looked at it like that before!" and comply with their wishes.

Imagine the scene going like this:

"Well these others (broccoli and salad) taste funny."

"They don't taste funny to me. Just try them for once. I'm sure your stomach is going to be just fine. All we want is for you to be healthy."

"You know, you're right, Dad. How silly I've been. I'm sorry for giving you guys a hard time, when you're always doing stuff for me. I'm sure my stomach will be OK, and maybe I'll even learn to like this."

Right.

There are several other reasons why it's important to put an end to pretend talk. First of all, pretend talk takes a child's focus away from where it should be: cooperation. Second, fake conversations almost invariably aggravate kids (and everyone else), thus making the likelihood of compliance much lower. And third, these counterfeit dialogues confuse children by implying that Negotiation is an option for them when it really is not.

4. Picky Peter: Let your child decide

Once they made up their minds and stated their case (one repeat is OK), Peter's mother and father kept quiet and let their son decide what he was going to do.

> "I'm done."
> "You only finished two things."
> "Well these others taste funny."
> "OK, but the deal is no dessert. We have ice cream bars tonight."
>   (State the case)
> "Aw, come on. That's not fair!"
> "That's our deal." (State the case)
> "I'll eat more chicken and noodles."
> Silence. (Stop talking, let your child decide)
> "Well this 'new deal thing' is really stupid!"
> Silence. (Let your child decide)
> Grumbling to himself, Peter leaves the table.

After Mom and Dad stop talking, which of the four choices of frustrated children will Peter pick? Negotiation is out, so that leaves testing or noncompliance (sneaking an ice cream bar later). Peter chooses testing, in the forms of Butter Up and Intimidation. As we'll see in Chapter 13, parents can respond to testing by either making no response or by using consequences. Here Peter's parents do well by making no response. Peter now can either leave the table—without dessert—or up the ante by testing more or engaging in noncompliance. We'll deal with both of these possibilities later.

Once you've made up your mind, stated your case and stopped talking, it's not always easy to wait to see which choice your frustrated youngster is going to make. What can you do to pass the time? Actually, you usually don't have to wait that long, but here's what you need to be thinking during those often-tense moments. First, brace yourself. Plan how you will respond if you get testing (further talking by the child will constitute Badgering at this point) or noncompliance (Chapters 13 and 14). If you think testing and manipulation is likely, try to predict which type the child will use as well as any tactic switching that might occur. You might anticipate, for example, "He'll probably start out by pouting and when that doesn't work, he'll throw a full-blown tantrum." By anticipating this behavior you'll be ready for it.

On the other hand, you might anticipate that you could get cooperation and you need to be prepared to respond positively to that.

5. Picky Peter: Respond to your child's choice

You've made up your mind, stated your case, stopped talking and let your child decide what he is going to do. How do you respond to the child's choice? It's fairly simple:

Child's Choice	Parent's Response
Cooperation	Positive reinforcement
Negotiation (no longer an option)	No response
Testing and manipulation	No response or consequence
Noncompliance	Consequence

Cooperation should be reinforced by praise. "Why didn't you do that the first time I asked?" is not positive reinforcement. "Thanks for doing what I asked" is. Being a parent means dealing with your own emotions and being able to turn that switch inside yourself depending upon what your kids do. In parent-request or child-request situations where kids are frustrated, a parent's attitude needs to be determined-but-not-angry.

In our example, Peter tests and manipulates, in the hopes of getting an ice cream bar. His parents say nothing. Peter then leaves the table. Mom and Dad handled their son well—firmly and gently.

Clinical Trial: Rapid Rita

Let's apply our five steps to the Case of Rapid Rita.

1. Rapid Rita: Should we negotiate?

You recall that Mom had decided that she couldn't let her daughter have a kiddie cart, but that she was still going to bring Rita shopping with her. Though her decision requires some courage, Mom is determined. Mom's decision also means that getting a kiddie cart is now a non-negotiable item.

2. Rapid Rita: State your case

Mom and Rita are getting out of the car on the first shopping trip under the New Regime. Mom tells her daughter that she will not be able to get a small cart this time. Rita seems to have no reaction. Mom was afraid that might happen. She was hoping perhaps they could get the conflict out of the way in the parking lot, rather than in the store with a huge audience.

Sure enough, as parent and child enter the store, Rita sees the small carts:

"Mom, can I push my own cart?"

The moment of truth has arrived. Mom has decided she will state her case once more, then stop talking, get ready for the worst, and keep moving.

"No. You can't have a cart because you run with it."

Good. Clear, brief and firm response. Brace yourself, Mom!

3. Rapid Rita: Stop talking

"I promise I won't run. Please. Please!" (Butter Up, Badgering) Silence.

Mom says nothing, gets a big shopping cart and keeps moving into the store. She wants to get as far away from the kiddie carts as possible. Mom knows that at this point she can't control her daughter's mouth, but she can control her own. Whatever testing and manipulation she's going to get, she'll only make things worse by talking back to her daughter with useless demands, attempts at distraction or parental begging.

4. Rapid Rita: Let your child decide what to do

The ball is now in Rita's court. Her mother has made it clear what the deal is today. No kiddie cart—period. Mom's silence speaks louder than any words could. As expected, Rita chooses the testing option. But whereas Mom had expected to be faced with aggressive Badgering and a ferocious Temper, she encounters only a surprisingly passive Martyrdom from her daughter:

> "I never get to do anything." Rita pouts.

5. Rapid Rita: Respond to your child's choice

Mom remains quiet. "Can it be that my daughter is not going to try to make me look like a horrible mother in front of the forty thousand people in this store?" Yes, on this occasion it can be. Next time may be different (as we'll see later). But after her brief dabbling with Martyrdom, Rita seems to have forgotten all about the kiddie cart.

> "Mom, what can we have for lunch?"
> "How about hot dogs from Flip's?"
> "Yeah!"

The kiddie cart problem may not be solved yet, but Mom's off to a good start. When a parent has made up her mind, stated her case and stopped talking, children often sense the determined-but-not-angry attitude in the adult. Many times—though not always—sensing that attitude in the parent makes children drop the option of testing. After a brief try at pouting, that's exactly what Rita did—this first time around.

Clinical Trial: Moody Matthew

Now let's apply our five steps to the Case of Moody Matthew. You recall that Matthew's parents were concerned about their son's reaction to their periodic denial of his requests. After stopping to think the situation over,

Matthew's parents decided that (1) they would first listen respectfully to any request their son made, (2) they would then take time to think the request over, if necessary, and (3) they would give their son a clear response—once. After that they would no longer talk. This new system was discussed with Matthew, and his reaction was merely "Whatever."

Let's examine Matt's parents' problem, denying a child's request, in the light of our five steps.

1. Moody Matthew: Should we negotiate?

Imagine the situation is the same as it was before. Matthew wants to go see his friend's new game, but it's getting late in the evening and it's a school night:

"Mom, can I go to Bobby's?"

This one isn't too hard for Mom. She knows immediately what her answer will be. She also knows the issue is nonnegotiable. Her mind is made up.

2. Moody Matthew: State your case

Mom says what she needs to say. Her response is brief, clear and not ambivalent.

"No, dear, it's too late."
"But he's got that neat new game he wants to show me."
"Not tonight, Matthew. You can go tomorrow."

Matthew tries giving his mother some "helpful" information, but Mom repeats her request as clearly as she did the first time.

3. Moody Matthew: Stop talking

Matthew persists.

"Oh come on. Why can't I? It's just across the street."
Silence from Mom.

What else needs to be said?

4. Moody Matthew: Let your child decide what to do

The ball is now in Matthew's court. He can cooperate by dropping the subject, he can test and manipulate, or he might even consider sneaking out to his friend's. But active noncompliance is not really this child's thing. On the other hand, he certainly doesn't want to cooperate and give up. Matt chooses testing. He's been able to at least get a rise out of his mother on previous occasions:

"I never get to do anything!" (Martyrdom)

The ball is now back in Mom's court, but that doesn't mean she has to talk!

5. Moody Matthew: Respond to your child's choice

Mom knows talking will only make matters worse, so she remains quiet. She has already made up her mind and stated her case. She makes no response to her son as he continues his testing attempts:

"I never get to do anything!" (Martyrdom)
Silence.
"You let Marci go to Kristen's." (Badgering)
Silence.
"I promise I'll be back in ten minutes."
Continued silence from Mom.
Matthew also becomes quiet. He crosses the room and lies down on the couch, where his mother can easily see him. Folding his arms forcefully, he lies there sulking and staring at the ceiling. Mom sits quietly for a while, not looking in her son's direction. Then she gets up and goes in the kitchen for some coffee.

As we'll see later, silence isn't the only effective response to kids' testing and manipulation. But it is what Mom chooses to do here. Though not saying anything at all feels a little awkward, Mom does a good job and her silence gives a clear message that she's sticking to what she had said. Her firmness and resolve will help when it comes time to deal with other frustrating situations in the future.

The moral of these stories? When kid's are frustrated, impulsive parental talking can get you into big trouble. By being more aware of when to talk and when to stop talking, these moments of friction can be resolved much more efficiently. What do you do the rest of the time? Talk as much as you want and enjoy your kids! Listen to them and tell them stories. Ask them questions about what they think.

But you didn't really think Picky Pete, Rapid Rita and Moody Matthew were going to give up that easily, did you? Of course not! Kids are just kids. There will be plenty of times when testing and manipulation will pop up, and we need to make clear exactly what to do with it.

13

Take Charge: Testing and Manipulation

Y ou want to get along with your kids and you want your youngsters to learn self-control, or frustration tolerance, as they grow up. Therefore you try to prevent the unpleasantness of testing and manipulation by giving some thought to how you manage Start Behavior, Stop Behavior and turning down children's requests. You also avoid unnecessary and provocative talk when you are managing a mini-conflict situation, so that Negotiation doesn't become testing and so that testing, in turn, doesn't give rise to noncompliance.

Still, as all parents know, even when you are managing conflicts as well as you can, you will not be able to prevent all testing and manipulation. Sometimes kids just have bad days. They may be feeling more ornery because they're sick or because something went wrong at school. They may imitate a testing tactic they just saw a friend use.

So there will still be times when you must take charge in situations where you are confronted by Badgering, Temper/Intimidation, Threat, Martyrdom, Butter Up and Physical Tactics. In previous chapters we have given some hints about how testing can be managed. Now we're ready to tackle the problem head-on.

Four Principles

Here are the four basic principles we recommend to our parents for managing testing and manipulation:

> **1. Identify and label testing.**
> **2. Don't give in once testing has begun.**
> **3. Don't reinforce revenge.**
> **4. Ignore or consequence testing behavior.**

1. Identify and label testing

Before a parent or teacher tries to manage a specific mini-conflict situation, it's important to think clearly about what's going on. Testing and manipulation generally occurs as a response to parent requests (Start or Stop) or denied child requests, so adults need to be on the lookout under these kinds of circumstances. It's also important to keep in mind that every time a child expresses some negative emotion, that by itself does not mean that testing is occurring. The child could be physically hurt or upset with someone else, which calls for the warm, supportive side of parenting.

Correctly identifying testing as testing—and not as something else— also means that parents are thinking clearly. And thinking clearly means that an adult will not get so emotionally upset himself, and as a consequence he will be able to handle his frustrated child much more fairly and reasonably. Remember that testing and manipulation is all about emotion, not reason, and when kids are able to make their parents uncomfortable, parental mismanagement is often the result.

Once testing has been identified, it is a good idea to try to label the type of testing that is occurring. Is this behavior an example of Badgering or Martyrdom? Or is it Threat or Temper? Perhaps what I'm confronted with here is a combination. It's not so important to be absolutely correct about the testing label; certainly in some situations different interpretations are possible. The point is that identifying and labelling testing helps parents think realistically, stay relatively calm, and then decide what to do. Identifying and labelling testing also helps parents decide when to talk, when to keep quiet, and how to avoid pretend conversations.

Identifying and labeling testing is often the fork in the road (or the river)—miss the boat here and you're in for trouble. For example, Picky Pete's parents inform him that he can't have the ice cream bar because he didn't finish three of four dinner selections. Their frustrated son responds with:

"Aw, come on. That's not fair!" (Martyrdom, Temper/
   Indimidation)

The fork in the road. From here this mini-conflict can go two different ways, depending on how Mom and Dad think. What will happen if Mom and Dad don't think realistically and fail to identify and label Peter's Martyrdom and Temper tactic? If Mom and Dad think:

"This is ridiculous!! There's no reason for this behavior! We've got to make him understand!"

Then they'll talk, saying something like this:

"You hardly ate anything! What is your problem!? That wasn't the deal."

In which case, Peter will respond with more testing:

"Well this 'new deal' thing is really stupid!"
   (Temper/Intimidation)

And it's off to the races with another pretend conversation.

What if Mom and Dad, on the other hand, think realistically, identifying and labelling the testing, and—Robert Frost would be proud—taking the Road Too Often Less Travelled by Parents? Peter says:

"Aw, come on. That's not fair!"

Mom and Dad think:

"This is testing. Probably Martyrdom. That's to be expected in this situation. Peter's frustrated and he's still getting used to the New Deal. Don't want to give in to him, and we also don't want to make the situation worse by talking too much."

Then they either keep quiet or say something like this:

"You're still getting used to the New Deal."

This comment gives Peter a little sympathy, but it also tells him that his parents mean business—in which case, Peter might give up the chase, or he might respond with more testing:

"Well this 'New Deal' thing is really stupid!"
Silence from Mom and Dad.

At this point Mom and Dad will say nothing else. After a while, Peter will start getting the message that his parents aren't so manipulatable any more. Mom and Dad, in turn, won't feel like their son is running the house.

2. Don't give in once testing has begun.

As we saw earlier, before they started thinking things over, the parents in our three families were giving in to their active, frustrated and testing-prone youngsters. Peter got to leave the table without finishing his dinner, Rita got the kiddie cart, and Matt got to go to his friend's in the evening. No wonder these adults felt the kids were running the house.

The most obvious recommendation regarding testing and manipulation: *Don't give in once testing has begun.* There is no better way to insure that your kids will continue to act like little monsters whenever they don't get their way.

Though you don't have to be a rocket scientist to come up with this piece of advice, it's easier said than done. First of all, in a conflict situation you have to recognize that testing is occurring. That's not easy in the heat of battle. Next, you have to remember that testing is all about emotion and not about reason. For parents the hardest part about not giving in once testing has begun is this: *dealing with the uncomfortable feelings inside yourself.* Each type of testing and manipulation, you recall, is "designed" to create an unpleasant feeling inside the parent:

Testing Tactic	Unpleasant Feeling
Badgering	Weariness of repetition
Temper	Defensiveness

Threat	Anxiety
Martyrdom	Guilt
Butter Up	Guilt (later)
Physical Tactics	Fear

Once testing has begun, the child's deal—or offer to you—is: *Give me what I want and you can rid yourself of your unpleasant feeling. It's fast and easy! Don't give me what I want, and you can continue to suffer— perhaps even more than now.*

Fast and easy all right. Until the next time the youngster wants something. Then the same problem returns. The kid grows up running his parents' lives and learning zip as far as self-control is concerned.

Rita's mother learned all this at one of our workshops, and she began to realize that, no matter how difficult it was, not giving in to her daughter after testing had begun was a solid investment in the future welfare of both her daughter, herself and their relationship. As you recall, the first time these two went shopping and Mom drew the line about no kiddie cart, Rita surprised her mother by producing (1) only a weak martyr-like response and then (2) cooperation.

The next time Mom wasn't so lucky:

"Mom! Can I push a cart?"

"No."

"Why can't I?"

"Because you run with it. You'll be able to push a cart in another year or two."

"I wanna push my own one! I never get to do anything!" Rita starts crying loudly. Then she throws herself down on the floor, howling at the top of her lungs. To Mom it feels like a hostile grocery store crowd is gathering to watch the action.

Here's the fork in the road for Rita's mother. At this moment, on a scale from zero to 100, Mom's anxiety level is about 97. It would be so easy to give her daughter a cart to push. The hassle and all the embarrassment would end immediately—guaranteed. After all, there's no Dad to help her here. She's tired and has to go home to cook dinner. Just one little phrase, "OK, get a cart," will end the pain. It's already been a really long day....

Rita's only available parent stops herself in the midst of these thoughts. Somewhat reluctantly, she faces reality: "Give Rita what she wants when the girl is acting like this and I might as well turn in my Parenting Badge. It's testing and manipulation, primarily Temper, but there's also Badgering and Martyrdom thrown in. Not to mention an audience! Last time I was firm and she responded fairly quickly. After all, she's only four! Imagine what she'll be like if some day she treats her own kids this way! Nope, kiddo, there will be no cart today. The people in this store can think what they want, but you're *my* daughter."

Mom says nothing more and keeps moving, knowing that, no matter how angry the little girl is, she will not let her mother out of her sight. Rita follows along, but keeps screaming. It's extremely embarrassing. It takes the little girl three full shopping aisles to finally quiet down. Mom is able to complete her shopping.

No fun, but a solid investment in the future.

3. Don't reinforce revenge.

Does this job never end!? When frustrated kids are testing, it's hard enough not giving in to them. In conflict situations, that's often the biggest part of the parenting job, but not giving in isn't the whole story. You also have to be careful not to give the kids the satisfaction of revenge. The desire for revenge of some sort is a natural feeling that often occurs in human beings who are angry at someone else. There is nothing abnormal, inherently homicidal or extremely dangerous about this feeling. If you reinforce the revenge motive in your children as they grow up, however, you can wind up with bigger problems later.

How do you prevent your youngsters from being rewarded with a sense that they have successfully retaliated at you for your not giving them what they want? The answer goes back to two factors we have discussed before: not getting too excited and not talking too much.

Remember Difficult Dad and Difficult Kathy? Here are several of Dad's statements to his daughter during the course of their argument about her going to bed:

"You gonna move or am I gonna have to do it for you!?"

"YOU KNOW SOMETHING? I'M SICK AND TIRED OF YOUR
COMPLAINING ABOUT EVERY LITTLE THING YOU'RE
ASKED TO DO!"
"YOU WATCH THAT MOUTH OF YOURS, YOUNG LADY! I
WOULDN'T HAVE TO RAISE MY VOICE IF YOU'D DO
WHAT YOU'RE TOLD ONCE IN A MILLION YEARS!!"

Recall that Kathy is also a live wire, like her father. She's already
frustrated by his request that she retire for the night. She's mad at her
father. Do you think on some level she enjoys Dad's acting as though he's
being driven insane by her? Of course she does.

Both the loudness of a parent's voice and the intensity of the negative
emotion can communicate to children that the youngsters' reprisals are
sinking in and having a "good" effect. Sometimes, though, the simple
amount of talking can send the same message by itself.

Picky Pete's parents, for example, came up with their own version of
the Gettysburg Address:

"Sorry, but we don't have time to worry about your friends. The
person we do have to worry about is you. Now we weren't put on
this planet to torture you constantly, which is what you seem to
think. All we want is for you to be healthy by eating what you're
supposed to, and if you want, we can all sit here and wait for you
till the cows come home!"

Peter knows from this extensive monologue that, even though he won't
see any ice cream bar tonight, he did get back at his parents for trying to
starve him to death.

Moody Matthew's Mom came up with a somewhat shorter discourse,
entitled "On the Need for Childhood Reciprocation." It went something
like this:

"Listen. Don't we love you? Don't we do a lot for you? Don't we
give you most of the things you want? Then why can't you do
just this one little thing for us? Just for tonight. Huh?"

This verbal dissertation was shorter, but had a similar effect to that created by Picky Pete's parents' comments. Matt's mother's remarks tell her son that his Martyrdom is getting through to her. He has succeeded in creating a very uncomfortable feeling in his older and more powerful parent. Matt thinks to himself, "Here she is crouching down next to the couch and pleading with me. If I can keep up this feeling-sorry-for-myself thing just a few more minutes, I should be on my way to Bobby's for the rest of the evening! If she doesn't let me go, at least I got some payback for my frustration."

4. Ignore or consequence testing behavior

So far we've discussed what *not to do* about testing. Basically, don't reinforce either of testing's two goals. But what do you *do* about testing? Earlier we talked about making up your parental mind, stating your case, keeping quiet and letting your child decide what she was going to do. What if you've handled the situation well and you are still faced with testing and manipulation?

Once again the answer is fairly simple, but easier said than done. You will consequence some forms of testing and manipulation and you will make no response to others (taking charge does not always mean talking!). What you choose to ignore or consequence will depend on several things:

1. The aggressiveness or obnoxiousness of the child's response
2. The age of the child
3. Parental temperament: the eye of the beholder

1. The aggressiveness or obnoxiousness of the child's response

Often parents choose to make no response to what they consider to be the less obnoxious and more passive forms of testing. Many forms of Martyrdom, for example, such as pouting or whining, fall into this category. You don't necessarily have to do anything when kids pout, whine or give you the "silent treatment."

Many—but not all—parents would agree that the following statements from frustrated children might require no response:

"You're so mean!"

"I hate you!"

"I promise I'll never do it again!"

"You don't love me anymore."

"Why? Why? Why? Why?"

"I want it now!"

"I never get anything."

No response would have been a good strategy for Matthew's mother once she had made up her mind and stated her case:

"Mom, can I go to Bobby's?"

"No, dear, it's too late."

"But he's got that neat new game he wants to show me."

"Not tonight, Matthew. You can go tomorrow."

"Oh come on. Why can't I? It's just across the street."

No response from Mom.

"I never get to do anything!"

No response from Mom.

"You let Marci go to Kristen's."

No response from Mom.

Matthew also becomes silent. He crosses the room and lies down on the couch, where his mother can easily see him. Folding his arms forcefully, he lies there sulking and staring at the ceiling.

No response from Mom.

More aggressive or obnoxious testing from kids, however, should be consequenced. For example, children should not be allowed to hit their parents. Older children should not be allowed to swear at their parents or break things simply because they didn't get their way.

Consequences can include the temporary removal of something pleasant from a child's life or the addition of something unpleasant to a child's life. The possibilities are numerous:

- loss of part of the child's allowance (older kids)
- time out (approximately one minute per year of age)

- temporary loss of a toy
- monetary fine
- chores of varying difficulty
- loss of TV time
- loss of computer time
- bedtime fifteen minutes earlier
- parent withdrawal from scene ("reverse time out")
- going home early from an outing
- loss of a treat or a dessert
- loss of right to purchase something
- having to sit for a while during an outing

Consequences must be administered according to the same rules we just discussed for not reinforcing revenge: very little talking and very little negative emotion. "That's it. THAT'S IT! I'VE HAD IT!! That will be 25 cents off your allowance and bedtime will be fifteen minutes early tonight! When are you going to learn... etc, etc...?" A parent who administers a consequence like this will destroy the beneficial effect of the consequence.

Unless the child's behavior is very serious or objectionable to begin with, it is usually a good idea to warn a youngster that a punishment is forthcoming if the child continues to do or not do what the parent doesn't want. Matthew's mother, for example, might have used this approach:

"Mom, can I go to Bobby's?"
"No, dear, it's too late." (Makes up her mind, states her case)
"But he's got that neat new game he wants to show me."
"Not tonight, Matthew. You can go tomorrow." (States her case)
"Oh come on. Why can't I? It's just across the street."
"If you keep pushing me, your bedtime will be fifteen minutes
  earlier." (Mom identifies boy's testing, gives a warning)
"I never get to do anything!" Bobby leaves.
Mom does nothing else.

If Matt continued to push, Mom would inform him of the consequence:

"Mom, can I go to Bobby's?"

"No, dear, it's too late." (Makes up her mind, states her case)
"But he's got that neat new game he wants to show me."
"Not tonight, Matthew. You can go tomorrow." (States her case)
"Oh come on. Why can't I? It's just across the street."
"If you keep pushing me, your bedtime will be fifteen minutes
  earlier." (Mom identifies boy's testing, gives a warning)
"I never get to do anything!"
"Your bedtime is fifteen minutes earlier."
"That's not fair!"
Mom is silent.

What if the testing and manipulation, in the parent's opinion, is more serious, more obnoxious or way out of bounds right off the bat? Picky Pete's parents found his one comment very objectionable and they sent him to his room. But they did this in a very angry, emotional manner. The approach below would have been better:

"Dogfood's better than this junk!"
"You can take fifteen minutes in your room for your language.
  Now."

This statement is firm and minimizes any feeling of revenge Peter might get. Peter can finish his dinner after his "rest period." What if Peter refuses to go to his room? That's now noncompliance (next chapter).

2. The age of the child

A child's age can also play a role in how a parent responds to testing. A three-year-old who throws a huge tantrum on the family room floor doesn't necessarily need to be held down or sent to his room. A four-year-old who badgers all the way home about not wanting to sit in her car seat might also best be managed by no response. Many parents, however, feel that tantrums and Badgering in older children are inappropriate, so the adults are more inclined to consequence that kind of behavior.

Rita's mother felt her grocery store options were restricted because of the age of her child. Talking to the little four-year-old had been useless, and Mom didn't think that taking her daughter back out to the car for tantruming would do any good. So mother "just" made no response to her daughter's testing when the girl didn't get her way. (No response often requires a lot of guts!)

3. The eye of the beholder: parental temperament

There is a great deal of difference from parent to parent with regard to what kinds of testing behavior will be ignored and what kinds will be consequenced. In some families, for example, an eight-year-old's saying "I hate you!" would be considered very objectionable, and this comment would be punished. In other families the same comment would be ignored. Some of the differences among parents are due to these parents' value systems, and these differences must be respected. As long as they are not being abusive, these parents have a right to raise their children as they see fit. Parents are also more consistent when they are doing something that they believe in.

Other parental differences in disciplinary style are due to parental temperament. We earlier referred to Difficult vs. Gentle temperaments. The Difficult temperament was more the "live-wire" type: quick to respond, more emotional, less patient. The Gentle temperament we described as the more "laidback" type: slower to respond, less intense emotionally, more patient. Parents with Difficult temperaments are more prone toward abusive parenting, because (1) these adults have lower frustration tolerance and (2) even normal kids are often very frustrating.

This discussion leads to a vital question: When it comes to dealing with testing and manipulation, what should a parent with a Difficult temperament do—ignore more or consequence more? And what about parents with more Gentle temperaments—how should they manage testing?

The answer may surprise you. Difficult parents (you know who you are!) should be more aggressive and consequence more—consistently and reasonably—when faced with the testing of their children. "In between" tactics, such as Badgering, Temper and Threat, for example, which other parents might choose to not respond to, should more often be consequenced by live-wire adults. Why? Because these adults will find these child behaviors more than just a little irritating, and with Difficult parents strategies that require no response and much patience will eventually break down. This breakdown, in turn, can produce emotional and physical abuse. A Difficult parent needs a strategy that is quick, assertive and effective—and at the same time reasonable and fair.

What about more Gentle parents? These people can do what they want, provided they are not pushovers for their kids when the children are testing.

1. IDENTIFY & LABEL TESTING.

2. DON'T GIVE IN.

3. DON'T REINFORCE REVENGE.

4. IGNORE OR CONSEQUENCE TESTING.

14

Take Charge: Noncompliance

As we saw before, testing and manipulation is an attempt by a frustrated child to get her way by influencing her parents' emotional state. The child is still accepting parental authority, but she is hoping that by making her parents uncomfortable (anxious, guilty, tired), Mom and Dad will perhaps change their minds and grant her wish.

That's what happens when testing is working for children. Peter's parents let him leave the table without finishing his dinner, Rita's Mom gave her daughter the kiddie cart, and Matt was allowed to go to Bobby's. Ultimately these acts take place with the blessing of parental authority.

What if Peter simply left the table without finishing, Rita just grabbed a cart and started running through the store, or Matt quietly slipped out the window to his friend's? These actions would be examples of active noncompliance, which involves rejection of parental authority. In these instances the children would simply be doing what they wanted to without considering any attempts to manipulate their parents. As we saw before, active noncompliance in young children is not unusual, and it is less worrisome because the little kids are still learning the basics of how to behave. As the kids get older, however, active noncompliance becomes more worrisome. Research shows that, as a child grows up, the longer aggression and active defiance persist, the poorer the prognosis—and the more miserable family life becomes.

Passive noncompliance in children can also be aggravating, but it is less worrisome. When children passively noncomply, they may really still accept parental rules and authority, but they often genuinely forget to respond according to those rules. Unlike active noncompliance, where a child's goal is often *to be defiant*, passive noncompliance usually involves another, non-defiant goal or just plain absentmindedness. For example, Peter genuinely hates broccoli. His main goal is not to defy his parents. And Karen gets so involved playing at her friend's house that she forgets to come home in time for dinner.

In either case, it's very important to deal with noncompliance effectively when children are young. We just saw that you prevent testing and manipulation by trying to do things that ensure cooperation from kids in the first place, and by knowing how to talk (or not talk) to your kids when the children are frustrated. Accomplish those two objectives and there will be less testing. Yet even when you are managing a situation as well as you can, you will still need to deal directly with testing from time to time.

All of the steps discussed in previous chapters apply to preventing noncompliance: designing strategies that foster cooperation, knowing when to talk and when to keep quiet, and managing testing and manipulation efficiently. Accomplish those three objectives and there will be less noncompliance. But—just as with testing—you will still need to manage active and passive noncompliance from time to time.

Here are several basic steps for dealing with active and passive noncompliance:

1. **Think realistically.**
2. **Consequence noncompliance.**
3. **Restructure for cooperation.**
4. **Reinforce compliance.**

These steps are similar to those we've discussed earlier.

1. Think realistically

When it comes to managing noncompliance, two parental attitudes are important:

> 1. Kids are just kids.
> 2. Active noncompliance is usually a more serious problem.

The first idea we have seen before. When kids are just being kids, they will present many different problems to their parents. That's part of the parenting job. Some of these problems will be problems with Start Behavior: Kids won't always do the good things that their parents want them to do. But if you think realistically about it, have you ever heard of a child who wanted to clean his room? (There are a few, but they're unusual.) And why should a child *want* to do homework? Or go to bed or pick up after himself? Most children don't naturally desire to accomplish these things. Kids have to be trained and motivated by parents to do them.

The same is true of Stop Behavior problems. Often children naturally want to do things that adults don't want them to do. Brothers and sisters, for example, frequently and spontaneously fight and argue with one another. It's a national pastime. Kids also naturally scream a lot and run around more than their parents wish they would. Children are great noise makers. Noise may be unpleasant for adults, but it comes from kids being kids. The argument here is not that it's wrong for parents to intervene if Mom or Dad feels there's too much fighting or too much noise. The argument is that parents shouldn't automatically think that these behaviors are horrible, unbearable or indicators that something is wrong.

2. Consequence noncompliance

When child noncompliance does occur, there should usually be a consequence meted out by a parent. Consequences should be greater for behavior that parents consider to be more serious or more obnoxious. Sometimes consequences can be tailored to the situation. Consequences should not, however, be accompanied by parental tantrums or lectures.

Peter, for example, didn't finish his dinner. That's a Start Behavior problem, an example of passive noncompliance. It's a small problem— not the end of the world (nor the end of Peter) by any means:

"I'm done."

"You only finished two things."

"OK, but the deal is no dessert."

"I don't want anything else anyway."

Peter leaves the table.

Peter's parents give a consequence: no dessert. They draw the line, state their case, stop talking and let their son decide what he wants to do. Mom and Dad do not lecture, they do not ask any silly questions, and they do not verbally attack their son. Since in this example these adults are thinking clearly, they do not get excited. Peter decides to leave the table without dessert.

Moody Matt, however, after his mother told him he couldn't go across the street to his friend's house, sneaks out anyway. This is more serious. This behavior is an example of active noncompliance, and Matt's evening escapade will receive a larger consequence than simply no dessert. Mom sees Matt coming back from Bobby's and she meets him inside the back door:

"You went to Bobby's after I told you you couldn't."

"Mom, I only went for a few minutes. It was no big deal."

"I'm afraid it is a big deal to me. I'm very concerned when you do
  something I specifically ask you not to do. This weekend I will
  give you a four-hour chore to do. You'll start working on it at 9 a.m.
  sharp."

"Mom, that's not fair! I only went to Bobby's for five minutes!"

Mom says nothing else. She turns around and leaves.

This was excellent work by Mom. Not only is she thinking on her feet, but she's exercising firm emotional self-control. She knows when to talk and when to keep quiet. Maybe the issue will be discussed again later, but it should't be discussed a lot during this potentially explosive moment. Since she means business but remains calm, the consequence Mom meted out above will have good effect.

By contrast, how effective do you think the same consequence would be if Mom dished it out under these circumstances?

"Why did you go to Bobby's after I told you you couldn't?"

"Mom, I only went for a few minutes. It was no big deal."

"I asked you a question!"

"I don't know."

"You don't know. How sweet. That's really great. WHAT KIND OF ANSWER IS THAT!? Did your IQ suddenly drop to 25!"

"I just wanted to see his new game. He wanted me to come."

"I don't care if the Governor and the President wanted you to come!!"

"Don't start yelling at me."

"You did something I specifically asked you not to do. DO YOU UNDERSTAND ME!! This weekend I'm giving you a four-hour chore to do. Believe me, I'm going to find something you'll absolutely hate! You'll start working on it at 9 a.m. sharp."

"Mom, that's not fair! I only went to Bobby's for five minutes!"

"Don't you try telling me what's fair, young man! Get out of here. I don't want to even look at you!"

Some parents answer that the second Mom response is more fitting, because what the boy did was more serious. These parents are dead wrong. In the second example, when he leaves the encounter with his mother Matthew is both humiliated and angry. If active noncompliance is something this lad has an inclination for, the last thing he needs—as far as his future welfare is concerned—is more anger and revenge motivation added to the fire. Bad job by this mother.

3. Restructure for cooperation

Whenever parents face recurring compliance problems, it's time again to stop and think. Something is not working. We've got to come up with a new plan of action. When noncompliance is repeated, there is no future in simply *expecting* a child to cooperate, and there is certainly no future in repeating parental tactics that obviously don't work.

Since our focus in this book is primarily testing and manipulation, we do not have the space here to discuss all the possible tactics parents might use when designing new responses to active and passive noncompliance. Here are two other books that can help:

For Start Behavior problems (passive noncompliance), such as getting up and out in the morning, eating meals, going to bed, doing homework and picking up, *1-2-3 Magic: Effective Discipline for Children 2-12* discusses a number of strategies that parents have found useful. For Stop Behavior problems (active noncompliance), *1-2-3 Magic* describes both "counting" for minor Stop Behaviors (arguing, yelling, teasing, sibling rivalry) as well as the Major/Minor System for more serious Stop Behaviors (lying, breaking things, stealing). *1-2-3 Magic* is available in both book, video and audio formats.

For preteens who show continued problems with serious noncompliance, Russell Barkley's book, *Your Defiant Child: Eight Steps to Better Behavior*, helps parents understand the motivations of oppositional children and then proposes, among other things, a concrete token system for parents to use employing consistent rewards as well as mild punishments (consequences). Like *1-2-3 Magic*, Dr. Barkley's program is a down-to-earth, no-nonsense approach which is also available in a video form called *Managing the Defiant Child: A Guide to Parent Training*.

4. Reinforce compliance

A critical step in dealing with noncompliance is remembering to reinforce cooperation. As we have mentioned before, when kids are acting up a lot, Moms and Dads are often so angry so much of the time that they never even feel like praising or rewarding their children. When difficult kids are finally induced to cooperate, the feeling these exhausted parents have is more like "It's about time!" rather than "Thank God!"

"Thank God!" is the better attitude. Kids' cooperation needs to be reinforced verbally so it will continue:

"Thanks for doing that."
"Wow, you did it the very first time I asked!"
"Great job on that homework!"
"You were a real whiz getting up and out this morning!"
"You really seem hungry tonight."
"You're making my job a lot easier."
"Way to go!"
"Good job, buddy."

Kids' cooperation can also be reinforced in other ways. Children who are regularly noncompliant often have trouble cooking up the internal motivation to do what they're supposed to. Therefore they often benefit from more potent and more frequent rewards, which can include many different possibilities:

- going out to eat
- time playing a video game
- staying up past normal bedtime
- TV time
- computer time
- video rental
- special meal, food or dessert
- sleep-over or having a friend over to play
- small purchase
- doing something one-on-one with parent
- points that can be spent on rewards
- poker chips that can be spent on rewards

These rewards should be administered in a consistent fashion. Rewards should be small enough so that they can be used frequently, and also so that they do not require exorbitant amounts of either parental funds or parental energy. Giving children some choice over which rewards they will earn at a particular time is also a helpful idea.

Your Relationship with Your Child

The overall nature of the relationship between a parent and a child also has considerable effect on the potency of both the rewards and the consequences which that parent attempts to use with that child. If the warm side of the parenting equation is nonexistent, the effect of any positive or negative consequences will be greatly reduced.

For example, if Matt's mother is not in the habit of frequently praising her son, listening sympathetically to him, and having fun with him, the weekend chore she assigned for his going to Bobby's will have much less effect. A parent who is a good disciplinarian cannot be a disciplinarian one hundred percent of the time.

So don't neglect the warm side of the parenting equation. Do enjoyable activities with your kids, grant a lot of their requests, goof around with them, talk to them. Enjoy your youngsters now, because they'll be gone a lot sooner than you think.

15

The Efficiency of Counting

In *1-2-3 Magic: Effective Discipline for Children 2-12*, we introduced a discipline procedure known as counting. In one sense, counting—or what is often referred to as the "1-2-3"—is as old as the hills. Parents have been doing it for years. But most parents have not been doing it right. In *1-2-3 Magic* we took several important steps toward perfecting the procedure so that it was gentle, fair and effective.

Counting is simple, but applying it is not always easy. It is basically a "three strikes and you're out" type of operation. For example, when a child is engaging in an annoying behavior, such as arguing, whining, interrupting, teasing, fighting or tantruming, a parent gives a warning by holding up one finger and saying, "That's one." The parent then pauses to let the child decide what to do. If the child stops the undesirable activity, the parent might praise the youngster for cooperating. But if the child hits a 2 and then a 3, there is a consequence which is usually administered immediately. The most frequently used consequence is a rest period or time-out—approximately one minute per year of the child's age. Other consequences, however, can also be used in place of time out. These consequences might include some of those we've discussed before, such as a fine, loss of a privilege, earlier bedtime, etc. Consequences can be made larger or smaller depending upon the seriousness of the offense.

The basics of the counting procedure are always explained to the children before the 1-2-3 is started. Any questions the kids have are also answered.

Counting is remarkably effective, but only when the procedure is used properly. There are several important requirements for the 1-2-3 to work efficiently:

1. When using counting, no extra talking is allowed. As we have seen, extra talking distracts a child from his basic task: cooperation. Superfluous chatter also irritates the very kids who are being "encouraged" to cooperate.

2. When using counting, adults should remain as calm as possible. Like extra talking, extra emotion from adults during conflict situations distracts children. Not only that, but many kids take emotional belligerence from their parents as a challenge to fight, rather than as an appeal to cooperate.

3. Counting is most effective when trying to elicit child compliance when that compliance requires only a short period of time. In other words, counting works best for terminating Stop Behavior (stopping an obnoxious behavior takes only one second or so) and for helping encourage Start Behavior that takes only a couple of minutes (such as feeding the dog, brushing teeth, or picking up a coat). Counting may be less effective for tasks like homework, getting up and out in the morning, cleaning rooms and going to bed, since these activities require more than just a couple of minutes.

4. Given these facts, it follows that counting can be remarkably effective for not only most kinds of testing and manipulation, but also for some kinds of active noncompliance.

Could counting have been used with Picky Pete, Rapid Rita and Moody Matthew? Yes, if you stop and think about it. Let's take a look.

Counting Picky Pete

Since eating dinner is a Start Behavior that takes a while, Mom and Dad probably would not want to use counting to get their son *to* eat. (Some parents claim they have done this successfully, however.) Counting could be used, though, if Peter got into testing after his parents informed him— under their New Deal—that he would not be getting any dessert. Here's how it might go:

"I'm done."

"You only finished two things."

"Well these others taste funny."

"OK, but the deal is no dessert. We have ice cream bars tonight."

"Aw, come on. That's not fair!"

"That's the deal."

"Well this 'new deal thing' is really stupid! All my friends think you guys are weird. No one else I know has a big plan for how they eat their dinner."

"That's 1."

Peter's comment, "Well this 'new deal thing' is really stupid!, etc, etc," is fairly aggressive and disrespectful, so here Mom and Dad choose to count his defiance—rather than to ignore it. Most parents would probably agree that his comment should not simply be let go. Unfortunately, most parents would also respond to Peter's obnoxious words with an obnoxious, superficially-educational comeback of their own, such as "Now that's no way to talk to us, young man. Is that the thanks you give us for simply trying to make sure that you grow up healthy?" To which Peter might respond, "I'd rather die than eat this junk anyway." And the race would be on. What would we have here? Another pretend conversation.

Keep in mind, though, that ignoring less offensive forms of testing is a legitimate option. For example:

"I'm done."

"You only finished two things."

"Well these others taste funny."

"OK, but the deal is no dessert. We have ice cream bars tonight."

"Aw, come on. That's not fair!"
"That's the deal."
Peter pouts.
Mom and Dad say nothing.

Here Peter's passive Martyrdom tactic, pouting, is simply ignored by his parents. What's the hardest part of this strategy for mothers and fathers? The hardest part of successful ignoring is (1) not letting yourself feel guilty first, then (2) not getting angry at your child for "making" you feel guilty, and then (3) not talking as a result of the guilt and anger. Not an easy task by any means! But with practice, these mental and emotional gymnastics can be mastered. Think clearly—and keep your mouth shut!

Less obnoxious testing tactics are sometimes repeated by children to the point that the behavior becomes much more aggravating simply because of the repetition. This is often the case when the kids are using Badgering that is persistent but not especially angry. Here's how Peter's parents might handle mild-mannered testing that becomes irritating because of its repetitiveness:

"I'm done."
"You only finished two things."
"Well these others taste funny."
"OK, but the deal is no dessert. We have ice cream bars tonight."
"Aw, come on. That's not fair."
Silence from Mom and Dad.
"I'll eat more chicken and noodles."
"That's not the deal."
Peter pouts.
Mom and Dad say nothing.
"I don't like this stuff. It makes my stomach queasy."
"That's 1."
"Why can't I have an ice cream bar?"
"That's 2."
Peter leaves the table.

This strategy by Peter's parents is simple and to the point. It is also gentle but effective. Counting here prevents a mini-conflict from becoming a maxi-conflict. Ten minutes later, Peter and his mother might be enjoying listening to a ball game together. Or Peter and his Dad might be heading out to the store. An extended pretend conversation, however, could have ruined the whole evening, made both parents depressed, and might have provoked them into thinking their son needed a shrink.

Occasionally parents object to the counting procedure by telling me: "In the last example, the parents start counting their son without even having the courtesy to explain to him what he was doing wrong. How's the boy ever supposed to learn from that?" The answer is: Unless Peter is less than three-years-old (Peter was in second grade), it is highly unlikely that he is unaware of the times when he is pushing or testing his parents against their will.

In fact, one of the benefits of counting is precisely this: Counting makes the kids *think about what they are doing* that their parents don't like. "That's 1" to a child means (1) I'm doing something I shouldn't be, (2) I'd better figure out what it is, and (3) I'd better stop it. This isn't rocket science. It *is* an exercise in children learning self-discipline! But there is nothing wrong with necessary or useful explanations. We tell parents: If you really believe that your child doesn't understand what he's doing wrong, then by all means explain the situation to him—clearly, briefly and firmly.

When used properly (without a lot of excess excitement and chatter), counting is a very efficient disciplinary technique. Counting helps parents identify and label problem behavior. In conflict situations counting is also a way for parents to make up their minds, state their case, stop talking and let their children decide which of the four choices the youngsters want to engage in.

Counting Rapid Rita

As you recall, Mom's problem with her cute but overly-speedy four-year-old was a Stop Behavior problem: running with the kiddie cart. Stop Behavior like this can be counted, so the 1-2-3 is another alternative Mom can use with her daughter in the grocery store.

Here's how it might go. As the two enter the store, Mom explains to Rita that she can have a cart, but may not run with it. Mom tells Rita that the third time she runs with the cart, she will lose it. Mom also remembers that it is important to praise compliance, so she will be on the lookout for times when Rita is walking with the cart and Mom will praise that behavior.

Rita is walking next to her mother and pushing her little cart.
"Rita! I'm so happy you're walking with your cart."
Five minutes later, Rita sails past the fresh produce at about 40 miles per hour.
"Rita, no running. That's 1."
Rita walks once again.
"Thanks for slowing down, honey."

Mom gives a warning, a short explanation and then praises her daughter's cooperation. That's all the talk that's needed. Rita cooperates for the moment. That does not, of course, mean that this girl will slow down for the rest of her life.

What if Rita hits a 3? You know the answer to that! Mom would say, "That's the third time running, so you lose the cart." Mom would then take the cart away and prepare for her daughter's testing. If Rita pouts, Mom can ignore that tactic. If Rita tantrums, Mom can count the explosions, or can institute an immediate rest period in a corner or bathroom of the store, or back in the car. Many children respond well to that procedure, but only if the parent keeps quiet while doing it.

Counting Moody Matthew

The testing behavior Matthew employed in our earlier example could be counted or ignored. Mom handled the situation well when—instead of talking—she simply did not respond to her son's manipulative efforts. Here's how she might have used counting:

"Mom, can I go to Bobby's?"
"No, dear, it's too late."
"But he's got that neat new game he wants to show me."
"Not tonight, Matthew. You can go tomorrow."
"Oh come on. Why can't I? It's just across the street."

"That's 1."
"I never get to do anything!"
"That's 2."

Crisp, gentle and to the point. Mom's counting in this case tells her son that his mother has made up her mind, that the issue is not negotiable, and that further testing and manipulation will be consequenced.

For a more complete description of the counting precedure, as well as answers to Frequently Asked Questions, consult *1-2-3 Magic: Effective Discipline for Children 2-12*.

Part V

Practice, Practice, Practice

16

Ready for Anything! Part 1

If you feel your children are running your life, it's going to take plenty of practice to turn things around. If you feel your children are training you rather than vice versa, it's going to take commitment, guts and a solid knowledge of what to do to get things going in the right direction. It helps parents to know what other Moms and Dads have been through in the process of gently but firmly taking charge of their own households. In this chapter we'll take another look at an earlier situation, and in the next chapter we'll look at the experiences of a number of parents.

Badgering

Eight-year-old Tommy and his mother, Theresa, are from Chicago. They are visiting Theresa's sister in Minneapolis. Tommy and his mother have always wanted to see the Mall of America. Tommy wants to see the roller coaster and his mother wants to see the stores. So on their first morning Aunt Emily takes them to the Mall.

Things go well until Tommy sees the roller coaster. He goes nuts with excitement.

"Mom, can I go on it? Mom, can I go on it?" Theresa doesn't think these rides are safe; she's sure she's heard of people being killed on them. And she certainly doesn't want to ride on the thing, but that would mean her son would have to go by himself.

"No, not today, dear," she replies weakly. As soon as the words leave her mouth, she realizes that her response just implied that she might consent to letting him go some other time. And that in turn implied that she was not totally against his going on the ride in the first place.

Tommy appreciates all this in a heartbeat. The floodgates are opened.

"Mom, just this once! Just this once! Just this once! Mom! Just this once! Just this once! Mom, Mom! Just one time! Just one time! Mom, just this once!" His voice is rising and getting louder. Some passersby are smiling knowingly. Others are scowling. If Mom doesn't let him go, there may be hell to pay—in front of all these people. If she does let him go, she'll be terrified he'll never come back alive.

"Mom! Mom! Just one time! Just one ride, that's all. Mom!!"

What to Do: Make Up Your Mind!

We left Mom in a quandry before—definitely caught between the devil and the deep blue sea. Her son is all over her about riding the roller coaster. Her attempt to draw the line in response to the boy's request is weak, which opens the door for Tommy's energetic testing. Her statement, "No, not today, dear," violates most of our criteria for making a good denial of a child's request. Although the denial is brief, Mom's statement is unclear, reeks of mixed feelings, and gives absolutely no explanation.

What should Mom do? Mom first needs to Make Up Her Mind! That's not easy to do when your son is right in your face, but here are the steps we outlined before:

Make Up Your Mind!
1. Label the problem behavior.
2. Identify what is not working.
3. Change your thinking from wishful to realistic.

4. **Choose or restructure.**

5. **Anticipate your child's reaction.**

1. Label the problem behavior

The problem here is the possible denial of a child's request as well as testing and manipulation, Type 2, Badgering, by an excited little boy. Mom must not only make a decision, but then she must manage her son's reaction to her decision—all with an audience only a few feet away.

2. Identify what is not working

What is not working here for Mom is a weak denial of her son's request. Her weak denial arose directly from her indecisiveness about Tommy's riding the roller coaster. Mom is going to have to Make Up Her Mind.

3. Change your thinking from wishful to realistic

Tommy's testing is obnoxious but perfectly normal. It will not go away until Mom makes a decision.

4. Choose or redesign

Mom decides to buy some time to think. She tells Tommy: "Tommy, I'm not sure yet if I want you to go on this ride. I need ten minutes to think it over. We'll walk around a little bit and then I'll give you an answer. But if you bug me during that time—even once—then the answer is no."

5. Anticipate your child's reaction

Mom needs to anticipate several things here. Will her son shut up for a few minutes to let her think it over? If he does, fine. If he does not, Mom will have to tell him the roller coaster is out because he bugged her during her reflection time. Then she'll have to anticipate he'll get into some major testing—most likely a tantrum, and she'll have to plan to manage that.

Mom thinks the whole thing over for a while. Miraculously, Tommy leaves her alone, but she can tell he's still chomping at the bit. Mom finally decides that they wouldn't have roller coaster rides in shopping malls if the rides killed every third youngster who rode them.

> "OK, Tom. I made up my mind."
> "Yeah?"
> "You can go on the ride, but try to find an adult or somebody older to sit with you in the car. I'll get sick if I go on that thing."
> "OK! YES!!"

End of problem and, except for one petrified mother, a good time was had by all. Mom's pause for thinking time also was a good move because it meant that Tommy's energetic Badgering was not immediately reinforced by the granting of his request.

As soon as Mom made up her mind to grant her son's wish, the problems of stating her case, not talking, letting her child decide what to do, and responding to Tommy's choice all became non-issues because the problem was over. But you can't always give your children what they want. So let's turn these non-issues back into issues by playing this scene out with a different script.

A Different Script

In the opposite scenario Mom says "No" to Tommy. She is not going to let him ride the roller coaster. If this Mom is going to say "No" to this little boy, she'd better know how and when to talk. The steps we discussed before were these:

Stop Talking!
1. Should we negotiate?
2. State your case.
3. Stop talking.
4. Let your child decide.
5. Respond to your child's choice.

1. Should we negotiate?

Mom thinks the problem over. She knows there are parents who would let their kids go on these things. But she is simply not comfortable with the idea. If there were someone else whom she knew who could ride with him... but there isn't. Mom has made up her mind and she is not going to negotiate with her son regarding his safety. She feels bad for Tommy. He'll be very disappointed and she'll feel very guilty. There will be hell to pay—but she has decided. She braces herself.

2. State your case

> "Well, Tom. I made up my mind."
> "Yeah?"
> "I'm not letting you go on the roller coaster. I don't think they're safe. And I want to make something clear. I know you're going to be very disappointed, but I'm not going to talk it over with you."

Mom turns and starts walking toward the next group of stores.

3. Stop talking

Mom just did. Can she keep it up?

4. Let your child decide

The ball is now in Tommy's court. As expected, the boy is extremely angry. Tears of rage roll down his cheeks.

> "That's not fair! Just give me one good reason why I can't go!! JUST ONE!"

Mom can tell that her son is just warming up. What is she going to do?

5. Respond to your child's choice

The "choice" of this frustrated child on this occasion is testing and manipulation. Tommy is both disappointed and furious. His mother is guilty and anxious. In the midst of the coming emotional hurricane Mom needs to try to recall the procedure for managing testing. That's why practice is important: When you're upset, your mind becomes forgetful and it's easy to fall back into primitive and ineffective parenting behavior.

Tommy's Testing and Manipulation

Earlier we discussed four steps that are necessary for handling testing:

Take Charge: Testing and Manipulation

1. **Identify and label testing.**
2. **Don't give in once testing has begun.**
3. **Don't reinforce revenge.**
4. **Ignore or consequence testing.**

The unpleasant scene at the mall continues:

"Look at all those other kids. They're my age, aren't they!?
   WELL, AREN'T THEY?"
Mom keeps walking.
"Answer me! You didn't give me a good reason!!"
Silence from Mom.
"What do you think I am—a baby!?"

1. Identify and label testing

This is tough stuff. Tommy's testing tactic is now a combination of Badgering, Temper and Martyrdom. Mom does her best to remind herself that this is normal behavior in frustrated children. Her son is a good kid. He is not a demanding brat. Still, she wishes she'd never come to the mall.

2. Don't give in once testing has begun

Many different voices are screaming inside Mom. One voice is telling her to let her son ride the roller coaster. "What's the big deal? You're just being a worry wart. Other kids are riding the thing and they're not dead."

Letting him take the ride would end all this unpleasantness immediately. Another voice is saying "Talk to him, calm him down! Use that active listening business." Mom thinks of different active listening phrases: "You're really upset with me for not letting you take the ride," or "This is really hard for you," or "I know how frustrated you must be." But somehow all these attempts at sympathy seem to miss the intensity of the moment, and such comments at this point feel to her cheap and condescending. Another part of Mom knows full well—from past experience—that words such as these will only reveal her own mixed feelings, and consequently make her son's testing worse.

Mom concludes she is stuck. Tommy will calm down whenever he calms down, and her best contribution to that process will be to keep quiet and not indicate in the slightest that she is ambivalent about her decision.

3. Don't reinforce revenge

Although Tommy is normally not a vengeful kid, in this situation he'd like nothing better than to get back at his mother. His tirade continues:

> "This is so stupid, I can't believe it. Three-year-olds can ride the idiot roller coaster, but not me. No, I'm a BABY! Babies can't go on dangerous things like that! They might get themselves hurt. That must be why they built the roller coaster, so they could kill as many people as possible. But they won't get a chance to kill me, because I'm a BA-BY."
>
> Mom remains silent.

Mom continues to bite her tongue. Anything she says is likely to feed her son's anger. There will be other times for sympathy and listening.

4. Ignore or consequence testing

So far, Tommy's mother has decided to ignore her son's outburst. But she does make another decision. She decides to give it five more minutes, and if Tommy hasn't quieted down considerably by then, she will inform him that she will count further public displays of Temper. If Tommy hits a three, they will leave the mall.

Mom's warning becomes unnecessary as Tommy gives up his

shouting and reverts to an angry silence. Even though she is tempted, Mom makes no attempts at conversation, distraction or appeasement. She senses that even positive reinforcement (for calming down) would be dangerous at this point.

Tommy's mother did an excellent job under very trying circumstances. Keep in mind that whether or not roller coasters in general are safe is not the issue here. That decision is for parents to make with their own children. This mother made up her mind, stated her case, stopped talking and left the ball in her son's court. When he started his testing, Tommy's Mom was then forced to exercise considerable emotional self-discipline, both because of her son's behavior and because of her own upsetting feelings. She was tempted to give in, but that would have reinforced her son's obnoxious behavior. She was tempted to talk, but there was nothing she could say that wouldn't simply add fuel to the fire. Mom also could have had a ferocious tantrum of her own—a tempting alternative, but that would have reinforced her son's revenge motive.

Denying the boy's request, explaining her decision and then remaining slient was Mom's most legitimate—and most difficult—option. Giving in, talking or blowing up herself would all have been easier—for the moment. When dealing with testing and manipulation, parents often find that the most legitimate decision is the hardest one—and the one that requires the most self-control. A corollary of this idea is: *Just because you, your child or both of you are very upset does not mean that you have handled a conflict situation poorly.* Good parenting can be a tough business.

17

Ready for Anything! Part 2

Thank heaven there's more to raising kids than just having to deal with testing and manipulation all the time. Most parents do get lots of opportunities to enjoy fun things with their children, such as:

1. Cuddling up before bed reading a story
2. Watching the baby sleep
3. Taking the kids to Disney World
4. Showing the baby to Grandma for the first time
5. Teaching the youngster how to ride a bike
6. Being needed

But to enjoy the pleasant aspects of parenting, you have to be able to manage the difficult times efficiently. So... back to the salt mines!

1. Debate Team Candidate

Eleven-year-old Jeff asks his father:

"Can I go out after dinner to play?"
"No, you still have homework to do."

"I'll do it when I come back in, right before bed."

"That's what you said last night and it didn't work. Remember?"

"Oh, please Dad. I promise!" (Badgering, Butter Up)

"Get your homework done first, and then you can go out. If you work hard, it shouldn't take more than a half hour."

"Why can't I just go out now!? I'LL DO MY STUPID HOMEWORK!" (Intimidation)

"I just got done telling you why!"

"I can't wait to grow up so I can go in the army. It's got to be more fun than living in this dump." (Martyrdom, Intimidation)

"Yeah, well wait till you have kids of your own some day—we'll see how big you're talking then!"

Comment: Bad news—pretend conversation. When trying to manage this child, which of our four steps does Dad need to think about ? Dad needs to consider the ones that are checked below:

Make Up Your Mind!
√ **Stop Talking!**
√ **Take Charge: Testing and Manipulation**
Take Charge: Noncompliance

Dad's first comment, "No, you still have homework to do," was fine. He had no trouble making up his mind what the limits were going to be in this situation. But Dad's second comment, "That's what you said last night and it didn't work. Remember?" was not only weak but invited trouble. This comment implies that Negotiation is an option when it is not. Dad treats his son's testing as if it were a real effort at conversation, and as if the frustrated boy were going to respond to calm reason: "Gee, Dad, you're right. It didn't work that way last night. What a fool I've been! I'll go up and start my homework right away!" Jeff is testing, using Badgering and some Butter Up, and Dad gets caught up in a pretend conversation.

The good news is that only testing has occurred so far. Noncompliance has not been an issue.

Let's do this scene again:

"Can I go out after dinner to play?"

"No, you still have homework to do."

"I'll do it when I come back in, right before bed."

"You've got to finish your schoolwork before you play."

"Oh, please Dad. I promise!" (Badgering, Butter Up)

"E.O.D. (End of Discussion) Now you can waste time by hassling me or you can start your homework."

"Why can't I just go out now!?"

Dad says nothing.

Dad draws the line well here. He says "No" to the boy's request, while at the same time he makes a request that his son do his homework. Then Dad recognizes testing, signals the end of the conversation, and sticks to his words by keeping quiet.

Another consideration in this example: a regular task like homework should have a consistent routine and consistent rules attached to it. The job should not be open to discussion and renegotiation every night. For example, the rule might be that you start your homework at 4 and finish it before dinner. No TV, computer or play till after it's done. During the evening you then can do whatever you wish (see *1-2-3 Magic*, Chapter 17).

2. Intimidating Second Grader

Let's take another look at a situation from Chapter 1. Mrs. Menoni had this to say about her first encounters with one of her new second graders, Loren:

"I got to know Loren last year because of confrontations I had with him on the playground and in the hall. Loren would play roughly with other children, often teasing and even bullying them. Even though I would be careful in confronting him with his inappropriate behavior, he would become very upset. Sometimes he would throw himself on the ground, put his fingers in his ears, close his eyes and refuse to interact at all."

"Other times, when confronted, Loren would simply have a temper tantrum. He would yell at the top of his lungs that I was mean, unfair and had no right to criticize him. Defiance was written all over his face, and he was doing his best to intimidate me. It seemed his reactions were the worst when he didn't expect my confronting him—when my negative feedback, in other words, caught him off guard."

"I was at a loss for what to do. If I confronted him, I produced a tantrum. But I also couldn't let him get away with what he was doing to the other kids."

Comment: When trying to manage this child, which of our four steps does Mrs. Menoni need to think about? All of them:

√ **Make Up Your Mind!**
√ **Stop Talking!**
√ **Take Charge: Testing and Manipulation**
√ **Take Charge: Noncompliance**

Mrs. Menoni is caught in a Loren-style version of the devil and the deep blue sea. She can't let the boy get away with what he is doing to the other children, but she also does not relish having to confront one of his tantrums. The first thing this teacher needs to do is to make up her mind and not let herself be intimidated by Loren's possible (or probable) reactions to her requests. When she mentions that she was "careful in confronting him" she was probably making a mistake, because her ambivalence about a possible confrontation would very likely be reflected in the tone of voice or the language of her request. "Loren, don't you think you should be nicer?" is a much weaker request than "Loren, stop the teasing—now."

Imagine that on Tuesday, May 4, at 1:45 p.m., Mrs. Menoni makes a clear statement to Loren that he is to stop bullying and teasing. At this point Loren can cooperate, test and manipulate or not comply and continue the undesirable behavior. Negotiation is not an option here for the boy; his teacher is not going to negotiate *how much* he is allowed to tease or bully.

If Loren stops the obnoxious behavior, his teacher needs to praise him for his cooperation. If he tests in his usual fashion by blowing up (testing tactic Type 2), there should be a consequence. Temper tantrums in school situations are not only inappropriate behavior, they are also upsetting to the other children. The consequence might be removal from a playground situation as well as loss of another privilege during the day, detention after school, note or phone call home, or whatever else the teacher and school feel is appropriate. Loren should not be lectured about good and bad behavior; talking here will do little good.

What if Loren continues bullying or teasing? This would be straightforward noncompliance, and the same consequences as those mentioned above would apply. Loren would be removed from the playground, physically if necessary.

3. Another Tale from the Trenches

We saw this example before:

"My daughter was about eight-years-old and wanted to spend the night at a friend's house whom I didn't approve of. I told her she couldn't do it. I was cooking dinner and she came into the kitchen and announced to me that she was going to stand there and watch me until I changed my mind. I simply told her that she had inherited her stubbornness from me, and she could stand there until midnight if she wished. I was not going to change my mind. She stormed off to her room and never said another word about it."

Comment: When trying to manage this child, which of our four steps does this mother need to reconsider? Only the ones checked below:

Make Up Your Mind!
Stop Talking!
Take Charge: Testing and Manipulation
Take Charge: Noncompliance

In other words, this mother handled the situation just fine! Mom made up her mind that her daughter could not go to her friend's house, and apparently the issue was also non-negotiable. Next Mom did a good job of recognizing her daughter's testing right away. Of course, the little girl pretty much announced that she had arrived in the kitchen with the express purpose of testing and manipulating her mother. Not many kids are so straightforward! Mom firmly but gently informed the frustrated youngster that testing and manipulation would serve no purpose. If the little girl had not stomped off to her room, Mom would have needed to be careful that she didn't get baited into a pretend conversation.

4. Potential Runaway

Here's another situation to revisit with our new insight: It is a hot, steamy day in mid-July. Six-year-old Jimmy is outside in the backyard playing with his dog, Sally. Dad checks out the window and notices that his son is spraying the dog with the hose. Though Jimmy is laughing hysterically, the dog is not enjoying the routine. Unable to escape because she is on her chain, she would rather be anywhere else in the Western hemisphere.

"Come here, Sally. Come here, Sally." Squirt. Laugh.

Dad yells out the window, "That's enough, Jim. She doesn't like that"

The boy does stop—temporarily. But several minutes later Dad hears his son's laughter. Looking out the window again, Jimmy's father sees that the poor dog is drenched. Jimmy is now squirting the animal in the face. The big Lab, generally good natured, is growling. Dad is mad.

"Get in here—right now!" Dad yells. "No!" Jimmy responds. Dad runs out into the yard, grabs his son by the arm, escorts him into the house, and sends him to his room. Both Dad and Jimmy are furious.

Ten minutes later Jim stomps into the family room and announces that he is running away from home.

Dad, still angry himself, says, "Fine!"

Jimmy goes upstairs and packs a small suitcase with some clothes and a toothbrush. Dad watches—saying nothing—as his son noisily drags the suitcase down the stairs, throws it out the front door, and then slams the door behind him. Dad peeks through the curtains. His son is sitting on the sidewalk next to his suitcase. The sun is getting higher in the sky and the temperature—already well above 90—is continuing to rise.

After about fifteen minutes, Jimmy reenters the house and declares, "I couldn't leave because you won't let me cross the street!"

Comment: Dad did very well in this example. His initial request, "That's enough, Jim. She doesn't like that," was clear, not ambivalent and gave an explanation. Dad's next request, "Get in here—right now!" was a little too emotional, but certainly didn't lack clarity or forcefulness. Jimmy's response was noncompliance, so Dad did the appropriate thing. He escorted the boy from the yard and sent him to his room for a time out. Jimmy hadn't killed the dog or done anything really horrible, so this punishment was a reasonable one.

Jimmy, however, is not about to take this consequence lying down. He threatens to run away from home (testing tactic number 3). What could his motive possibly be, since he knows he's not going to get his way and be able to continue torturing the dog? The answer is simple: it's the second goal of testing, revenge. Dad is going to be punished for his unreasonable restrictions on innocent fun.

Again, Dad handles his son's threat fairly well. Perhaps Dad should not have blurted out his angry "Fine!" in response, but he still does a good job of ignoring his son's manipulative effort. Jimmy finishes up with "I couldn't leave because you won't let me cross the street!", a matryrlike comment again designed to punish. If Dad avoids administering a long lecture to his son and disregards that statement, the whole incident will probably be over.

Dad could also have used counting when Jimmy was squirting the dog. If Dad had wanted to use the 1-2-3, he would have initially called out the window:

"Don't squirt the dog, Jim. She doesn't like that. That's 1."

What would that comment have accomplished? Several things. It would have told Jimmy that Dad had made up his mind, that he meant business, and that the issue was not negotiable.

6. Young Carpenter

Here's a new example to consider: Eight-year-old Ken asks his mother if he can use his Dad's electric jigsaw.

"I don't think so. You better wait til Dad's home."
"Oh come on, Mom. I know how to do it."
"No, I think it's too dangerous."
"There's nothing else to do." (Badgering, Martyrdom)
"I said 'No.' "
"THAT'S STUPID!" (Intimidation)
"When are you going to learn to take 'No' for an answer?"
"When are you going to learn that I know how to use the jigsaw?"
  (Intimidation)

"Just who do you think you're talking to, young man!?"

"Do you see anybody else in the room but you?"

"That's it! Get up to your room until I tell you to come out!"

Comment: Back to the drawing boards! Mom did a fairly good job of initially drawing the line and denying her son's request, though her comment was a little wishy-washy. But then she didn't recognize Ken's testing when it started. Instead, Mom got caught up in an aggravating fake conversation. Mom missed the boat when she said "I said 'No,'" undermining her position by trying to set the limit for the third time.

Let's do this one over in a different way. In our reprise of this scene, Mom will consider talking the issue over with her son. She'll focus on the two items checked below:

√ **Make Up Your Mind!**
√ **Stop Talking!**
   Take Charge: Testing and Manipulation
   Take Charge: Noncompliance

Reprise:

"I don't think so. You better wait til Dad's home."

"Oh come on, Mom. I know how to do it."

"What makes you think you know how to do it?"

"Cause I've done it with Dad watching me plenty of times."

"And he lets you do it all by yourself?"

"Yeah."

"Well, how about you do it and I watch you?"

"OK."

Here Mom takes more time to make up her mind and she also allows for the issue to be negotiated. And, in the end, she and her son have a good time together.

7. The Cold Shoulder

Let's take a final look at eight-year-old Kelly. She is annoyed because she was denied the opportunity—by her mother—to go out in the cold and ride her scooter. Kelly thought it was quite warm enough outside. Adding to the injury was the fact that her mother then denied a second request: the right to have candy within an hour of dinner.

Kelly marches into the kitchen, where her mother is sitting, and announces: "I never intend to eat again when you call me for dinner." After her proclamation, she turns, and without saying another word, she strides purposefully to her room.

Sure enough, when Kelly is called for dinner at 6:15, she does not appear. She is normally a very good eater. The family—Mom, Dad and Kelly's two younger sibs—proceeds without her.

Kelly persists until eight o'clock. At that point she suddenly appears and announces to her mother, "I'm ready for my dinner."

Comment: Kelly's parents handled this situation well. As mentioned, most kinds of Martyrdom can be ignored. That's just what was done here. Parental statements such as "You'll eat what I tell you to eat!" or forcing the girl to sit at the dinner table would only have made matters worse.

What should Mom do when Kelly says "I'm ready for my dinner."? Not serve her! Getting Kelly's dinner for her would be like reinforcing testing and manipulation, since the little girl still seems to be in a sullen, martyrlike mode. Kelly should be told where the food is and instructed to serve herself, eat and clean up afterwards.

In situations like this, the other necessary skill parents need to exercise is the ability to *not* start feeling guilty. Even in the face of ridiculous manipulative attempts like the one above, some parents do wind up feeling a little bit guilty—after all, their child is not eating! If the parent's guilt shows—whether through their attempts at conciliation or through angry defensiveness, the second goal of testing, revenge, will be reinforced. If that happens, this child will be more inclined to use that "successful" tactic in the future.

8. The Case of the Absent-Minded Mom

Ten-year-old Michelle and her mother are standing in line at their neighborhood convenience store. Mom wants to buy a Sunday paper. Michelle starts walking over toward the coolers and Mom says:

"No, honey, don't go over there."

Michelle keeps walking and temporarily disappears behind the displays. Mom says nothing, appearing lost in thought. In just a few seconds Michelle returns with a can of pop. The girl puts it down on the counter in front of her mother. Mom says nothing and pays for the pop along with the paper. The two then leave the store. Neither seems upset.

Comment: Not a big deal, but not a good job of parenting either. In this situation Mom would have done well to have considered two things:

√ **Make Up Your Mind!**
Stop Talking!
Take Charge: Testing and Manipulation
√ **Take Charge: Noncompliance**

If Mom didn't want her daughter to leave her side, Mom should have backed up her request, "No, honey, don't go over there." Michelle's action was an example of simple, though active, noncompliance. And unfortunately, Mom actively reinforced her daughter's noncompliance by purchasing the pop for the little girl.

How could Mom have backed up her request? One alternative would have been for Mom to count her daughter:

"No, honey, don't go over there."
Michelle keeps walking away.
"Honey, that's 1."

Does Michelle know what's she's doing wrong? Of course she does. With counting, the girl would also understand that Mom means business and that there will be a consequence if she doesn't cooperate.

On the other hand, Mom might not have really cared that much if Michelle wandered around the store or if she wanted to get some pop. In that case, Mom's making up her mind would have meant not blurting out, "No, honey, don't go over there," in the first place. If you are going to give an instruction, you want to mean business; otherwise it's better not to say anything. You don't want to innoculate your kids against listening to you.

9. Interior Decorator

Going out in public with small children can be risky business. What should be done with our young spraypainter? Five-year-old Bobby and his Dad are picking up a few items at their local superstore. Dad is a little nervous taking his son along, because the boy always seems to see a few thousand items that he wants immediately. Sure enough, Bobby spots a package of New Year's Eve party favors—the kind where you pull the string and confetti comes out. For some reason Bobby has really zeroed in on this item today. Dad has no idea how he even knows what they are .

Dad says no to his son's first request because he's afraid the party favors are dangerous and the boy will poke his eye out. But Bobby persists. His voice gets louder. Even louder Dad says "No!" and tells his son in no uncertain terms that that there's nothing more to talk about.

Dad continues to search for a pair of snub-nosed pliers. Just a few moments later his shopping is interrupted by a hissing sound and the scream of a store clerk.

"Hey! What are you doing?! Stop that! Who's kid is this?!"

Dad turns around to see his son holding a can of spray paint. The boy is waving his arms wildly as he sprays the screwdriver display yellow. Drops of paint are dripping from the screwdrivers onto the items displayed below.

Comment: What needs to be done here?

> **Make Up Your Mind!**
> **Stop Talking!**
> √ **Take Charge: Testing and Manipulation**
> √ **Take Charge: Noncompliance**

Whether you consider Bobby's action Physical testing (6) or active noncompliance, the first thing to do is to end the activity by taking the spray paint away from Bobby. There was no need for Dad to make up his mind or to decide how much to talk. Bobby's parents were charged over $50 for the damage their son caused, and they made their son pay for half of it from money he earned doing chores and from an allowance that they started giving him one month after the incident. Mom and Dad did not rant and rave at the boy, but their consequences made their point.

10. Cereal Seeking Sweetie

Remember the Andersen household? It's five o'clock and seven-year-old Janie is a little hungry:

"Mom, can I have a bowl of Lucky Puffs?"

"No, honey, it's too close to dinner."

"Oh please, just a small bowl. I promise I'll eat all my dinner."

"No dear, I don't think so. You know, you usually have trouble finishing your dinner, and this will just make it worse."

Big blue eyes look up at Mom out of an adorable little face. The child's hand gently rubs her mother's arm.

"Please, Mom. Please. I'll eat my dinner and I promise I won't even ask for any dessert."

The child is certainly a cute little creature. And she is usually cooperative, but sometimes her requests can be a little irritating.

"Honey, it's already past five o'clock," Mom says in a pleading tone.

"Just one small bowl, Mom? I'll eat my dinner."

Mom gives in, but she can't escape feeling as though she's been had.

"All right, young lady, but keep it small. And if you don't finish your dinner, don't come to me later telling me you're hungry, cause you're not going to get anything! Understand?"

Comment: In this scene thought needs to be given to these items:

√ **Make Up Your Mind!**
√ **Stop Talking!**
√ **Take Charge: Testing and Manipulation**
   Take Charge: Noncompliance

Butter Up may be less aggravating than the other testing tactics, but it is still testing. And, as this Mom discovered, it's also aggravating when you know you've been had. Can the little girl have cereal at five o'clock or not? This parent first needs to make up her mind. Is the issue negotiable? No. Then what needs to be done is to manage testing and manipulation.

Here's one way of doing this:

"Mom, can I have a bowl of Lucky Puffs?"

"No, honey, it's too close to dinner."

"Oh please, just a small bowl. I promise I'll eat all my dinner."

"No. You usually have trouble finishing your dinner."

Big blue eyes look up at Mom out of an adorable little face. The child's hand gently rubs her mother's arm.

"Please, Mom. Please. I'll eat my dinner and I promise I won't even ask for any dessert."

Mom says nothing else.

The ball is now in Janie's court. She can drop the issue. Or she can continue testing, possibly even switching tactics. In that case, Mom will either ignore or consequence the ploys her daughter chooses.

Here's another option for this parent:

"Mom, can I have a bowl of Lucky Puffs?"

"No, honey, it's too close to dinner."

"Oh please, just a small bowl. I promise I'll eat all my dinner."

"No. You usually have trouble finishing your dinner."

Big blue eyes look up at Mom out of an adorable little face. The child's hand gently rubs her mother's arm.

"Please, Mom. Please. I'll eat my dinner and I promise I won't even ask for any dessert."

"That's 1."

"Oh, come on. Please!"

"That's 2."

The message to Janie? You're doing something you shouldn't, you better figure out what it is, and you'd better stop.

Part VI

What Lies Ahead?

18

A Brighter Future

If you've decided that it's time to take charge of your home in a fair, gentle and reasonable way, then it's time to get started. No one benefits when one or more children run the house. Everyone suffers—mothers, fathers, grandparents, other siblings and relatives. And the child who is running the house now will find out later, much to his chagrin, that other people in the world don't like to be pushed around by anybody else's bad behavior. When he becomes an adult himself, this formerly demanding and aggressive child will discover that he has few friends and people avoid him.

Parents who consistently apply the principles described in *"I Never Get Anything!"* will find that, over a period of time, their kids' manipulative efforts will decrease—often dramatically. Parents and children will enjoy each other's company more, with the result that all family members wind up feeling better about themselves. Home will no longer be a war zone, but a pleasant place to be.

Of course, there are different routes to that happy ending! Once Mom and Dad decide they mean business, some children put aside most of their testing and manipulation efforts immediately. One couple, for example, came in to see me a few years ago because their four-year-old was having horrible tantrums several times a day. The couple was totally bewildered— not to mention worried—and they had no idea what to do. We discussed the fact that tantrums by frustrated children were normal, and I took Mom and Dad through all the steps of both preventing and preparing for this child's angry and manipulative efforts:

√ **Make Up Your Mind!**
√ **Stop Talking!**
√ **Take Charge: Testing and Manipulation**
√ **Take Charge: Noncompliance**

When Mom and Dad left my office, I felt they were ready for the challenge.

When this couple returned in two weeks, however, I was in for a surprise. Their son had had no tantrums—not even a single one—during the past fourteen days! The only explanation was that the little boy sensed something different in his parents: These adults meant business now; they were no longer going to be intimidated. Apparently I wasn't the only one who felt these parents were ready—their son did, too. We wish all kids would respond like that!

On the other hand, some children get worse when their parents put their feet down. These kids "up the ante" and severely test their parents' wills. Kids can get worse in three ways: (1) by escalating one particular testing tactic, (2) by switching tactics, or (3) both. With the kids who escalate, the tantrums may become more dramatic or the pouting or Badgering may last longer. It's as if the child is thinking, "Well, this tactic worked before, perhaps all it needs is a little tuneup; twice as much ought to do the trick."

Other kids switch tactics when they realize they are no longer getting their way. Children who used to employ more passive tactics such as Badgering, Threat, Martyrdom or Butter Up, for example, may switch to more aggressive methods like Temper or Physical Tactics. The most common switch in this regard is the "4-2" switch—Martyrdom to Temper. The child who used to pout (like Moody Matthew), starts blowing up when pouting no longer is effective. Such tactic switching, of course, partly expresses kids' anger at not getting what they want, but the change also signals a growing realization in the children that testing and manipulation is neither acceptable nor functional anymore.

If they are not prepared, parents can find tactic escalation and tactic switching bewildering and somewhat disheartening. Parents may think, "What are we doing wrong? The kids were supposed to be getting better—not worse!" Hang in there, because the opposite is true. Escalation and switching by kids are signs that adults are handling the situation well, rather than poorly, and the children are taking their final shot at trying to be the boss and run the show.

What if you, the adult, feel that you are doing everything you're supposed to, but things still aren't the way you think they should be? For example, you're making up your mind, stating your case, negotiating when appropriate, and managing testing as well as you can without having a fit or talking too much. The result is that the level of testing and noncompliance is better than it was before, but in your opinion it's still too high. If this is the situation, it's time to get a professional opinion. Get the name of a mental health professional from your doctor, from a friend or from a local mental health center.

The Future

Imagine two four year olds, Michael and Brandon, in two different homes. Let's assume that both children want Sugar Crisp cereal for breakfast and their parents get it for them. Let's then assume that both children change their minds when their bowl of cereal arrives, and they next demand Frosted Flakes instead. Naturally their parents resist the new requests, saying, "No dear, this is what you wanted." The denial of the second request next prompts each child to knock the bowl of cereal on the floor and erupt into a major fit of temper. Both children scream at the top of their lungs, become beet red and pound the table with both hands.

A defining moment for the futures of parents and children alike. Michael's mother calmly says, "That's 1." As Mom expects, Michael quickly hits a count of 2 and then he gets a 3. Mom escorts her son to his room for a short rest period. She says nothing. She knows children get like this sometimes, and though it's aggravating, Michael's just a kid. He continues his tantrum for a while and then becomes quiet. After he comes out from his rest period, the incident is forgotten. The boy eats some of his now-soggy breakfast, then heads happily off to preschool—no worse for the wear.

Brandon's father, on the other hand, becomes very upset after his son knocks the cereal to the floor. His Dad can't stand this kind of outburst. He doesn't know why his kid has to act like such a brat. Dad first tries to be firm. He explains that Brandon must eat what he requested and can't go around throwing his food on the floor. Brandon merely howls louder. His father now pleads, "Come on now, this is ridiculous!" He glances nervously at the clock. They must leave for preschool and the train in seven minutes. "All right, all right, just shut up! Here's your stupid cereal! And you'd better eat it all, pal!"

Brandon happily gobbles up his breakfast.

Upon visiting the two households a year later, we find that five-year-old Michael is learning "HFT"—high frustration tolerance—which will be an important part of his character. He is better—though far from perfect—at tolerating a "No" from his parents because their limits are fair and reasonable. He also knows they mean business. The home is generally peaceful, and Michael often spends time reading with his Mom and Dad. He's learning to recognize quite a few big words.

When we enter Brandon's house, however, we are greeted with screaming. It's Brandon vs. Mom this time. The child never seems to be able to take "No" for an answer. Brandon is learning "LFT"—low frustration tolerance—otherwise known as the Art of Pressing Your Parents' Buttons. The boy's temper is terrible, and often Mom and Dad just give him what he wants to avoid a battle. At other times, though, they don't feel he should be running the house, so they make periodic efforts to "outscream" him. Lately these yelling contests have resulted in his hitting them, and then—totally fed up—his parents occasionally spank him and put him in his room.

These parental temper tantrums leave Brandon's mother and father both feeling terribly guilty. They used to try to read to their son on occasion, but they quit because the boy was so "temperamental." Now, for the most part, they try to avoid him unless something absolutely has to get done. If this is what he's like now, they wonder, what's he going to be like when he's a teenager? What will he be like as a husband or parent?

These examples are not make believe. Thousands of similar stories—both happy and sad—are unfolding around you all the time in the community in which you live. There are millions of Michaels and Brandons in the world, and these kids are going to continue to doggedly act just like kids. The job of effectively managing youngsters' efforts to get what they want will always fall squarely on the shoulders of adults. When raising children, adults need to be both warm *and* demanding. With a basic understanding of testing and manipulation—and a ton of patience—parenthood can provide some of life's greatest satisfactions.